HUMANITY AT THE CROSSROADS

HUMANITY AT THE CROSSROADS

An Inter-cultural Dialogue

KARAN SINGH
and
DAISAKU IKEDA

OXFORD
UNIVERSITY PRESS

OXFORD

UNIVERSITY PRESS

YMCA Library Building, Jai Singh Road, New Delhi 110 001

)xford University Press is a department of the University of Oxford. It furthers the
University's objective of excellence in research, scholarship, and education
by publishing worldwide in

Oxford   New York

Auckland   Bangkok   Buenos Aires   Cape Town   Chennai
Dar es Salaam   Delhi   Hong Kong   Istanbul   Karachi   Kolkata
Kuala Lumpur   Madrid   Melbourne   Mexico City   Mumbai   Nairobi
São Paulo   Shanghai   Taipei   Tokyo   Toronto

Published in India
By Oxford University Press, New Delhi

First published 1988
Fifth impression 2003

ISBN 019 562215 4

Phototypeset by Taj Services Ltd., E 100–103, Sector VI, Noida, U.P.
Printed by Sai Printopack Pvt. Ltd., New Delhi 110020
Published by Manzar Khan, Oxford University Press
YMCA Library Building, Jai Singh Road, New Delhi 110 001

Preface

The two authors first met in February 1979, when Daisaku Ikeda was visiting India at the official invitation of the Indian Council for Cultural Relations, of which Karan Singh was vice-chairman at the time. In October 1980, Daisaku Ikeda extended a reciprocal invitation to Karan Singh to visit Japan. During this second visit, the amicable relationship between the two men deepened and they agreed on compiling a collection of dialogues.

Karan Singh, born the son of the Maharaja of Jammu and Kashmir in northern India, studied at the Kashmir and Delhi universities. His religious background is in traditional Indian Hinduism.

Daisaku Ikeda was born in Tokyo. He devoted himself to philosophical and religious activities as president of Soka Gakkai International (SGI), a laymen's organization professing faith in the Buddhism of Nichiren Daishonin (1222–82).

Although Nichiren Buddhism developed in Japan, it traces its origins back to India and Gautama Buddha. Over the centuries, Buddhism passed from India into China and then into Japan. In the process it divided into many sects. In his time, Nichiren Daishonin urged a return to the pure sources of Gautama Buddha more vigorously than anyone else. And in his efforts to do this, he created a highly original religious philosophy compatible with his own epoch.

As a citizen of the country where Buddhism was born, Karan Singh, though a Hindu, is nonetheless profoundly conversant with the philosophies and symbolism of the Buddhist scriptures. The dialogue between him and Ikeda recalls the source and the mouth of a great river. Though the two are separate, they are closely related and share much in common.

From an environment dominated by the philosophy of the Upanishads, derived from the ancient Vedas, the ultimate sources of Hinduism, Gautama Buddha produced the seed for a great spiritual culture which flourished in India and then spread its glory throughout most of Asia, including China, Tibet, Burma, Thailand, Indonesia, Korea and Japan.

Today, in India, Buddhists are few. Nonetheless, Gautama Buddha is still revered there as a sage, and the numerous places associated with him are regarded as sacred. It can be said that the Buddhist philosophical heritage remains deeply rooted in the minds of the people of India and of many other Asian lands.

Karan Singh and Daisaku Ikeda, though geographically separated, have discovered many points of affinity on deeper levels of thought and learning. They agree with special emphasis on the necessity of challenging and overcoming the crises invited by modern civilization, which has made astonishing advances in scientific technology to acquire vast power but has remained unable to break from the dominion of instinctive desires and impulses.

Transcending the differences between Hindu and Buddhist, both men are convinced that observation of the human mind and the development of wisdom to overcome instinct and blind impulse help humanity face all crises. This series of dialogues was born of that agreement. While pursuing the course of philosophical development from the Vedas, through the Upanishads, to Buddhism, the discussion casts light on the spiritual tradition underlying this development and shows how the civilization based on it can contribute to the welfare of modern humanity.

The specialist may find the treatment in this book somewhat cursory. It should be remembered, however, that the writers' aim has been to stimulate a greater awareness of the spiritual culture of the Orient and to awaken serious reflection about the true nature of humanity on the part of members of a civilization that has become entirely too technological and materialistic. It is the wish of both authors that this book may help awaken in the minds of their readers the determination to strive for the revival of a truly human spiritual civilization that will survive and flourish in the coming millennium.

KARAN SINGH

DAISAKU IKEDA

Contents

CHAPTER ONE

Sources of Indian Philosophy

1. Influence of the Indus Civilization on the Aryans

IKEDA: Japanese interest in India dates back to the middle of the sixth century, when Buddhism was introduced into Japan. Recently, fascination with India as a source of oriental culture in general is on the rise, not only in Japan, but in many other countries as well. Although I welcome this phenomenon as a stimulus to greater mutual exchange and development, I regret the lack of interest demonstrated in the Indus culture. Many people in Japan know that India's most ancient urban culture flourished over 3000 years ago in the region of the Indus River, in the northwestern part of the Indian subcontinent; but, apart from a handful of specialists, few attempt to study the civilization more deeply.

A number of reasons can be given for this neglect. Much remains uncertain about the origins of the Indus civilization. Furthermore, the Indus script, an all-important element in historical research, remains undeciphered. But apart from these relatively practical matters, I think it is essential to take into consideration a prejudice that many Europeans and Japanese bring to their study of Indian culture—an over-emphasis on Aryan elements. Since it began under European influence in the later part of the nineteenth century, Japanese study of Indian history has concentrated on the documents written in such Aryan languages as Sanskrit and Pali. Though Japanese scholars recognized the Indus valley civilization as having flourished before being destroyed by the Aryans, they largely overlooked its influences on later Indian civilization. But painstaking research since the discovery of actual historical sites in 1921, has gradually provided a fuller picture of this ancient culture and is beginning to point to intimate relationships between it and Aryan culture.

As an example I might mention the pipala tree depicted in clay seals and decorations of clay vessels excavated from Indus sites. This tree was later sanctified by Hindus and Buddhists alike. And some scholars claim that a personage depicted on seals unearthed at Mohenjo-Daro is the prototype of the Hindu god Shiva. Study of the Indus script reinforces the assertion that the creators of the Indus civilization were the forefathers of the Dravidians, who today mainly inhabit southern India. And this in turn lends credence to the idea that perhaps the Aryans did not destroy the Indus civilization and build a totally new and different civilization of their own on its ruins. Radioactive-carbon testing puts the final phase of the Indus urban civilization at about 1750 BC; that is, it was already declining before the invasion of northwest India by the Aryans (placed at about 1500 BC). In the light of these dates, the idea is gaining strength that the Aryans did not develop their own civilization in isolation, but borrowed from the Indus civilization— perhaps created by the forebears of the Dravidians—to generate a civilization that was in a sense an amalgam. Do you agree that this interpretation fits universal human cultural patterns better?

KARAN SINGH: It is true that the Indus valley civilization remains one of the great unsolved mysteries of ancient history. Although considerable work has been done on the decipherment of the numerous seals found at the sites, and two prestigious Jawaharlal Nehru Fellowships have been given to outstanding scholars in this field, a universally accepted decipherment has not yet been made. Until one is found, we can only speculate about the relationship between the Vedic and the Indus civilizations. Sir John Marshall maintained that there was a gap between the fall of the Indus cities and the Aryan influx, but later scholars led by Sir Mortimer Wheeler held the view that Harappa was overthrown by the Aryans and that the enemies mentioned in the Vedic hymns, who had great fortified cities, were in fact the people of the Indus civilization.

Given its high level of architectural and artistic achievement, especially in the field of town planning and urban development, it is clear that the Indus civilization must have flourished for many centuries. Apart from internal evidence within Vedic literature itself, especially frequent references to battles and prayers for victory, the point that you mention regarding certain figures and decorations on the Indus valley seals would tend to support the view that there was a definite interaction between the Aryans and the Indus valley inhabitants. Despite the confrontation between the two forces, certain universal symbols such as the bull and the tree are of continuing significance in Indian civilization. Moreover, the closely connected cults of the worship of the Mother Goddess and a figure that can be linked with Shiva Maheshwara tend to suggest a deeper link between the two civilizations.

Whether the residents of the Indus valley were Dravidians is still a matter for conjecture. It would appear that they were definitely darker than the fair-skinned Aryans, but this does not conclusively prove their Dravidian origin. In any case, the great genius of the Aryan people was the capacity to assimilate concepts from outside their own experience: 'Let noble thoughts come to us from every side', as the Rig Veda puts it. We can, therefore, assume that, if there was any interaction, the Vedic civilization did absorb the best features of the Indus valley people. Certainly more research needs to be done on this fascinating period when the contours of Indian civilization were being formed.

2. Early Aryan Society

IKEDA: Though at present it is difficult to draw a clear picture of the religion of the people of the Indus civilization, the immense volume of documentary evidence gives us a fairly complete idea of the religion of the Aryans who invaded northwestern India in about 1500 BC and gradually moved east to the holy river Ganga.

KARAN SINGH: First with regard to the chronology of the Vedic civilization, I may point out that it is not possible to date the Aryan influx authoritatively at 1500 BC. This is a complicated matter, and some views hold that the event took place at least 2000 years earlier.

IKEDA: As you say, this is a complex matter on which views differ. But without going into the difficulties of chronology, I should like to say a few words about my own observations of Aryan religious literature. As far as I have been able to discern, the ancient Aryans seem to have lacked tribal or ethnic religious faith. In contrast to the usual pattern—religions evolving from the most primitive state, the divinities of a blood-related group gradually becoming the gods of a tribe or people—in this case we already find an extensive pantheon in the Rig Veda, the most ancient of all Indian religious texts.

Of course, I am not implying that the Aryans were not divided into tribes. In early documents, like the Rig Veda, it is said that there were many Aryan tribes and that the head of each styled himself king. A king was assisted by *gramani* (chiefs of clans), *senani* (generals), and *purohita* (chief priests attached to the court). The *purohita* was especially important since it was part of his job to pray for victory in battle. It is said that such specialists in ritual were sometimes rewarded with treasure or cattle.

Whereas it is usual to find in primitive societies one person performing the functions of both king and priest, the sacrificial and ruling roles only gradually becoming separate, the two roles were clearly differentiated from the early stages of Aryan history. (This may even be a causative factor in the emergence of the Brahmans and their ascension to the pinnacle of the caste system.) How do you explain the apparent absence of a phase of tribal religious faith among the many tribes into which the early Aryans were divided? Did such a phase once exist? But documentary evidence of its existence is wanting at present. Is its apparent absence a characteristic of Aryan religion? Were the Aryans too occupied with their eastward advance toward the Ganga to develop a tribal religion? Or is there some other reason to account for its absence?

KARAN SINGH: The point that you raise regarding the absence of a phase of tribal religions can be answered if we realize that, in spite of their division into various clans and tribes, the entire Aryan people were knitted together by a powerful religious faith that involved worship of various deities and deified natural forces through fire oblations. The element that sets the Aryans apart from human history in many other parts of the world and that manifests their genius is their realization, from the very beginning, that all the great powers in the external world—the sun, the moon, the wind, the earth, the ocean, the rivers, the mountains, and so on—have parallels within human consciousness and are in fact manifestations of a single, all-pervasive divine force. It was this awareness of the unity of all existence that provided the greatest strength and vitality to the Aryan civilization and saved their religion from internecine strife with each tribe fighting for the primacy of its own deity.

As you rightly say, the role of the warrior and the priest were clearly differentiated from the early stages of Aryan culture. This does not mean that the priests had a monopoly on wisdom. In the Upanishads we find several instances of Brahmins going to the Kshatriya rulers for spiritual guidance. In daily life, however, the priests, who were in charge of the fire rituals of the Aryans, and the warriors, who were responsible for the protection and expansion of the tribe, were distinct but bound to each other in a creative symbiosis.

3. Development of Aryan Religion

IKEDA: In most parts of the world, religion began with tribal blood-relation faith, moved to faith in magic, and then entered the phase of pantheism and myth-making. The Vedic literature suggests, however, that this was not the case in

Aryan India. The Rig Veda consists of hymns to the divinities of heaven and earth and is followed by the Atharva Veda; which contains liturgical phrases for use in magical incantations. The later Brahmanas reveal a state in which the liturgical has gained the upper hand in religious matters. This course of development runs counter to the usual one.

Although the subject is open to various interpretations, I suspect that the severity of the climate and the nature of the land the Aryans encountered in their eastward advance across northwestern India may have influenced their religious development. The climate and ground were entirely unlike anything they had ever experienced before. In other words, the new environment may have prompted the Aryans to try to avert disaster and obtain happiness in one of mankind's most primitive ways: magical religious practices.

It is easy to imagine the perils and hardships the Aryans encountered as they cut their way through the dense jungles of the Ganga valley. When human beings' lives are in constant danger, it is difficult for then to sustain faith in bright anthropomorphic deifications of natural forces and their promises of blessings and joy. Instead, the direct diversion of disaster and obtaining of blessings become matters of the utmost urgency. I believe that the harshness of an unknown environment, which they were compelled to pioneer, caused the early Aryans to reverse the normal course of religious development from magic to polytheism and to move back from polytheism to magic. Some scholars account for this phenomenon on the basis of inclusion of indigenous religious elements. How do you interpret this stage in Aryan religious evolution?

KARAN SINGH: While geographical and climatic factors must indeed have been a major influence on the Aryans, I consider it incorrect to say that the Aryan religion moved from polytheism to magic. In fact, as I have pointed out, the religion cannot be termed polytheism at all because of the overriding awareness of the unity behind the various phenomena and forces symbolized by different divinities. The elements of what you call magic probably flowed from the absorption by the Aryans of a large number of indigenous cults that must have flourished among the original inhabitants of India. Apart from the Aryans and the Indus valley people, there must have been a number of comparatively primitive tribal groups, functioning at a lower cultural level, who, over the centuries, were absorbed into Aryan civilization. Many magical spells and incantations must have been aimed at averting disasters of various types, including virulent epidemics such as small-pox and other diseases for which there was no known cure. It is significant that such incantations are found largely in the Atharva Veda, which was compiled much later than the Rig Veda.

4. Vedic Gods

IKEDA: The Rig Veda, the oldest piece of Vedic literature, is filled with hymns to a large number of gods. From the predominance—about one-fourth of the whole—of hymns to Indra it is possible to judge the extent and importance of faith in this god. A deified realization of the Aryan ideal warrior, Indra was associated with thunder, and of immense size. He rode a chariot pulled by his famous horse Hari to destroy the fortresses of the Dasas, the Aryans' enemy.

KARAN SINGH: The predominance of Indra in the Rig Veda is indeed striking. The word Indra essentially means leader, and his deification clearly shows that the Aryans, who were engaged in life and death battles with their opponents, constantly exalted the power of the leader.

IKEDA: It is extremely interesting to note that Indra is thought by some to have evolved from a god worshipped in ancient Mesopotamia. The basis for this assumption is the appearance of the name of Indra, as well as the names of Mitra and Varuna, who occur later in the Rig Veda, in a treaty dating from the middle of the fourteenth century BC between King

Suppiluliumas of the Hittites (whose empire then controlled Asia Minor) and King Mattiwaza of the Mitanni. This evidence suggests that the origins of Indra and other Aryan gods may be very old indeed.

Indra belongs to the Buddhist pantheon of protective deities as well. He is said to dwell in the Palace of Correct Views in the Tushita Heaven on the pinnacle of Mount Sumeru.

I am interested in knowing whether Indra occupies a place of respect and importance in modern Hinduism or whether he has been overshadowed by Shiva and Vishnu.

KARAN SINGH: Whether Indra had any links with the Mesopotamian civilization is open to question; it seems more likely that there was a link with the ancient faith of Iran, which was projected by their great Prophet Zarathustra at about the same time as the early Vedas. Indeed the relationship between the Vedic religion and the Iranian religion of Zarathustra is a fascinating one. The Vedic hymns and the *gathas* of the Zend Avesta show a striking resemblance, and this is an area in which good deal of research needs to be done.

By the end of the Vedic period, the original Vedic Gods—Indra, along with Varuna and Mitra—had declined in importance and were replaced by the three major streams of later Hinduism—the worship of Vishnu and his incarnations, including Rama and Krishna; the worship of Shiva and his associates, including Ganesha and Kartikeya; and the worship of the Goddess in various manifestations. Indra is not an object of active worship among the Hindus today.

5. Devas and Asuras

IKEDA: The word *Deva*, employed since the time of the creation of the Vedas, has been used in India as a general term for god. Etymologically linked with the Latin word *deus*, it is related in meaning to brilliance or radiance. In Vedic literature the world *Asura*, which in later times was used to refer to demons, was applied to the gods themselves and, derived apparently from the name of the great Zoroastrian god Ahura Mazda, connotes such qualities as vitality and force. Though both Deva and Asura were applied to the Vedic divinities, they were used to represent different kinds of gods. Gods called Deva were usually benign, warm and familiar; whereas the ones called Asura possessed fearsome magical powers and were less attractive. This may explain why later the word Asura came to be used exclusively for wicked demons. In the case of Zoroastrianism, the cognates of the two words have had an interestingly different history.

In the gathas, the oldest part of Zarathustra's Avesta, the Zoroastrian holy texts, the word corresponding to Deva (*Daeva*) means a demon, whereas the one related to Asura (*Ahura*) becomes part of the name of Ahura Mazda, the paramount good god.

What is the modern Indian interpretation of these words? Asura is a difficult concept to understand in ordinary terms. Do the Indian people have a clear image of what Asura represents? If so, in what way is that image expressed?

KARAN SINGH: The relationship between the Deva and the Asura is indeed a most interesting one. As you rightly say, Asura was originally a term of respect, and this sense is preserved in the tradition of the Zend Avesta, where God himself came to be known as Ahura Mazda. The reversal of the meaning of the word Asura in the Indian context has not yet been fully explained. In the Pauranic tradition, the Asuras appear as rulers of great power and wealth, often far stronger than the Devas. Indeed there are numerous occasions in which a particularly powerful Asura defeats all the Devas and it is only by praying for the intervention of Vishnu, Shiva or the Goddess that he is finally defeated and the Devas restored to their original places.

In the Gita, Lord Krishna has clearly defined the Asuric characteristics as being full of insatiate desire, pride, arrogance, lust, and cruelty, while the Deva nature is described as containing all the good qualities of virtue, charity, kindness, and generosity. This would suggest that, at some point in the development of Hinduism, certain ruling classes set themselves up in opposition to the teachings of the Vedas and were only subdued with great difficulty. The case of Hiranyakashyapa is particularly interesting. He set himself up as God and destroyed all the statues of Vishnu in the temples. Finally he was killed by Vishnu in his incarnation as the man-lion Narasimha, who appeared at the request of the great devotee Prahlada, Hiranyakashyapa's own son. This would suggest that, while some of the Asuras were wicked, the whole race was not condemned and such outstanding devotees as Prahlada were born into Asuric families.

IKEDA: In Buddhism, the Devas of the Vedas become benign deities, called *ten* in Japanese, who assist in spreading the Buddhist faith and act as protective guardians. The most outstanding of them is Indra, or Taishaku-ten. The Asuras are thought to battle with the good gods—especially with Indra—and to dwell at the bottom of the great ocean surrounding Mount Sumeru, the central feature of the Buddhist cosmos.

In Buddhist philosophy, the words Asura and Deva have yet another meaning. Buddhism analyses the mental states of man into ten conditions, ranging from the lowest, hell, to the highest, Buddhahood. The fourth condition from the bottom is called Asura; the sixth, Deva (*ten*). Both are low states subject to inconstancy.

Although it originates in the Lotus Sutra, the pinnacle of Indian Buddhism, the doctrine of the ten conditions found later development and amplification in the work of the Chinese philosopher Tiantai (AD 538–97) and the great Japanese philosopher Nichiren Daishonin (AD 1222–82), who propounded the teaching that a single thought-instant can contain the whole universe (the doctrine is referred to as Three Thousand Worlds in the Single Thought).

KARAN SINGH: Your comments regarding the use of the terms

Asura and Deva in the Buddhist analysis are interesting. In the Hindu tradition, they can be said to represent the dark and the bright elements of the human psyche, respectively. While the Asuras have actually retained only a historical or mythological significance in Hinduism, the realization that each one of us carries within ourselves both the Asuric and the Daivic tendencies represents a major Hindu insight into the texture of human consciousness, which, incidentally has recently received considerable support in the West among Jung and his followers.

IKEDA: As you most astutely point out, each human being carries both bright, good, Daivic, and dark, evil, Asuric elements within the psyche.

I believe that doctrines of this kind indicate the superior thoroughness with which oriental thought has analysed the interior world of the human psyche and that this superiority accounts for the interest Jung, whom you mention, and such other leading Western intellectuals as the late Arnold Toynbee, have demonstrated in oriental wisdom.

The world of the psyche will be of the greatest significance to the future prosperity or decline of the human race, and people like you and me have the mission of transmitting the wisdom of the Orient as extensively as possible.

6. Duality in Indian Religion

IKEDA: In my several visits to India, I always have been struck by the dualities of asceticism and hedonism, denial and affirmation, calm and fervour that manifest themselves in Indian religion and the lives of the Indian people. If some Indians live as ascetically as did Vardhamana, known to his followers as Mahavira, the founder of Jainism, others take the utmost delight in the pleasures of life. People of the latter kind are well represented in Hindu religious festivals, loud with the sounding of cymbals and drums, ritual incantations of the names of the gods and frank celebrations of sexual love. The pessimistic view of life is illustrated by those who despise this world and its suffering and seek liberation from it through solitude, ascetic practices and mediation.

Though this duality is difficult for us to understand, some Japanese specialists in Indian studies have attempted interpretations. One such interpretation is the notion that spiritualism, asceticism and penance as a way of liberation from this life characterize the founders and preachers of the great Indian religions, whereas the hedonistic assertion of life and noisy fervour characterize the followers of these men and the way they express their faith.

Characteristic of all Indian religion is a hymn, or paean, to the universe and to life itself. I also believe that the differences in forms of worship and life-style apparent in Indian life are no more than the outcomes of different ways of discipline in the search for truth and different kinds of expression. For instance, viewed superficially, Buddhism appears to be a pessimistic religion since it sees this life as nothing but suffering, inconstancy, and selflessness. In fact, however, Buddhism is able to view life in this way because it is replete with a life-power giving limitless eternal abundance and joy and liberating and enlightening the human mind. In other words, it is possible to regard both the life of ascetic practices and meditation and the life of exuberant affirmation and celebration of sexual love as merely two different ways of praising the universe and life. When and for what reasons did the Indians come to manifest this dualism?

KARAN SINGH: The two streams of life affirmation and asceticism that you mention are major elements in most of the world's great religions. In Hinduism, from earliest times, certain people have given up the world to follow a life of ascetic renunciation either for their personal salvation or, as in the case of Prince Siddhartha, to find a way to universal salvation. This path of renunciation persists in Hindu society today; but, as far back as the Bhagavadgita, an attempt was made to unify the two paths. Lord Krishna in the Gita repeatedly says that it is not the outer but the inner renunciation that brings spiritual realization.

Differences in the various forms of Hindu worship are in fact the outcome of different forms in which the search for truth manifests itself. Hinduism does not insist that everyone follow exactly the same path; it makes allowances for the wide variation in temperament and inner tendencies among different types of people and provides a broad spectrum of approaches to the divine from which each individual can choose the one best suited to his own requirements. Indeed it is this great variety that gives continuing vitality to the Hindu civilization. Even in the present day you will find tremendous exuberance in various Hindu religious festivals, and a major programme of temple construction by Hindus in India and other parts of the world is at present under way. At the same time the tradition of strict monastic discipline persists too, as does the quest for the divine undertaken by individuals who are not attached to any religious denomination.

IKEDA: I see. Buddhism too has its pessimistic and optimistic aspects and in this respect is part of the current of Indian philosophical thought.

I firmly believe that the Lotus Sutra represents the ultimate height of the spirit of Mahayana teachings and the true essence of all Buddhism.

Viewed in the light of the teachings of the Lotus Sutra, the heart of Gautama Buddha's message is to impart to human beings the wisdom and life-force they need to live in positive ways. At first, Buddha hesitated to present this message in a straightforward way for fear that it would be misunderstood and would cause people to affirm the deluded, desire-driven, selfish lives they were leading at the time. Such affirmation would rob them of the desire to seek life on a higher plane. If his efforts were to have had an effect no better than this, Gautama Buddha would have done nothing different from the hedonists and worldly philosophers whose approaches held sway with many of his contemporaries.

Consequently, he first taught that life was to be rejected as suffering and strove to stimulate his followers to overcome completely their deluded, selfish, pleasure-seeking ways. Through such negative teachings, he wished to inspire people to turn a sceptical eye on the life of the present moment and to elevate their gaze to higher planes.

A segment of his followers, however—the Theravadins and the Hinayanists—failing to see his deeper meaning, stopped at a literal interpretation and developed their thought along negative, pessimistic lines. In their eagerness to flee from actuality and the society in which they found themselves, some of them went so far as to advocate destruction of the body, which they viewed as the source of delusion. Some held that the elimination of human wisdom is tantamount to enlightenment.

It was Mahayana—most of all the teachings of the Lotus Sutra—that halted this tendency, returned to Gautama Buddha's true intentions, and inherited the essential and universal spirit of Buddhism.

Mahayana teachings go beyond advocating a break with delusions. By evoking and manifesting the wisdom and force of life inherent deep in every human being, they strive to find the way to make correct use of the energy that informs even delusion. In Mahayana, the principle of converting delusion into the attitudes and actions of the Bodhisattva and of turning the suffering of life and death into the enlightenment of Nirvana is especially important.

Consequently, Mahayana runs neither to extreme asceticism nor to deluded, desire-driven hedonism but advocates instead the Middle Way. Not only does it represent to perfection the true Spirit of Gautama Buddha, it also produces what I am convinced is one of the loftiest religious spirits to be found in the history of humanity.

KARAN SINGH: Your comment that Buddhism appears to be, but in fact is not, a pessimistic religion, needs to be extensively propagated. The widespread impression is that Buddhism tends to take a negative, even masochistic, view of life by constantly stressing the element of suffering instead of the positive aspects of life affirmation. This interpretation finds compassion in Buddhism, but thinks it to be born of a negative reaction to life rather than a joyous evolution of divine consciousness. Your own very positive approach could go a long way in removing this impression.

7. Ancient Indian Religion and Modern Europe

IKEDA: When, about two centuries ago, the English became pioneers in European research into Indian religions, their main wish was to familiarize themselves with cultural backgrounds in order to maintain a firmer hold over colonial possessions. But, gradually, as they worked and translated, some of them became captivated by the depth and richness of their subject. Translations beginning with that of the religious poem Bhagavadgita and including the play 'The Recognition of Shakuntala' by the great poet Kalidasa, and the famous work from the second or first century BC, the Lawbook of Manu, made a great impression when they first appeared in Europe in the English language. When it was translated from English into German, 'The Recognition of Shakuntala' had tremendous impact on such people as Herder and Goethe. Nietzsche liked reading the Lawbook of Manu and drew his concept of the will to authority from it.

KARAN SINGH: You are correct in saying that western scholars, especially the English and the Germans, have, over the last two centuries, played a major role in the rediscovery of the Indian spiritual tradition. Apart from the names you have mentioned, I would like to add Max Müller and, later, Heinrich Zimmer, who wrote a number of brilliant commentaries on Hindu philosophy, mythology, and iconography. In particular, men like Professor Max Müller did remarkable work in compiling the Vedas for the first time in print. It is not generally realized that, until then, since its composition thousands of years ago, the entire corpus of thousands of Vedic hymns had been passed down from generation to generation entirely by memory, a mnemonic feat unparalleled in the history of mankind. We thus owe a deep debt of gratitude to the European scholars for their work.

IKEDA: We certainly do. Indian religious philosophy had influence in England and France, but it made its greatest impression in Germany: probably for a variety of reasons but almost certainly because the Germans found a mysticism akin to their own in it. In addition to Goethe, Herder and Nietzsche, whom I have already mentioned, Schopenhauer, Kaiserling and Hermann Hesse, too, were influenced by Indian religion. Schopenhauer discovered a core for his own philosophy in the Upanishads, which he read in Latin and which he praised as the most beneficial of all books and as his own consolation in life and death. Nietzsche rated Buddhism higher than Christianity and drew from it in the construction of his own philosophy. Wagner too was strongly influenced by Buddhism and attempted to express the idea of Nirvana in several of his operas. But the pessimism pervading much of the thought and art of these and other Germans suggests that they adopted only the darker, more ascetic elements of Indian religion. In this connection, it is interesting to notice that they and other Europeans alike adopted only the Theravada (or Hinayana) school of Buddhist thought.

KARAN SINGH: The Theravada School of Buddhism was introduced into Europe earlier than other schools because European scholars on the Indian subcontinent first came into contact with the traditions and texts in Sri Lanka (then known as Ceylon). E. Burnouf and C. Lassen published their essays on Pali, in French, in 1826; and in 1837 an edition of the first thirty-eight chapters of the Mahavamsha in Roman characters with an English translation was brought out by George Turnour. Later, again through India, European scholars of Mahayana Buddhism travelled to Tibet and China and introduced the great teaching to Europe.

IKEDA: In the emotional and spiritual vacuum following

World War I, Kaiserling introduced Mahayana Buddhism as part of the wisdom of the Orient and insisted that the teaching of the Bodhisattva, which he rated very high, was the sole way to change the world and inspire true reformation in mankind.

I too am convinced that the wisdom of the Orient as it manifests itself in Indian culture can play a vital part in the spiritual development of modern industrialized nations.

KARAN SINGH: Your point about the role that Indian culture can play in the spiritual development of modern industrialized nations, and indeed in saving the world from impending disaster, is one of my major preoccupations. Indeed, the whole eastern religious tradition, which includes Hinduism as well as Buddhism, has a tremendously significant contribution to make towards the survival and well-being of mankind in this nuclear age.

IKEDA: Many of the western intellectuals with whom I have engaged in dialogues have seen eye to eye with Oriental traditions, especially with Buddhism. And, in the following chapters, I should like to pursue in detail some of the topics on which agreement between East and West seems most promising.

CHAPTER TWO

Development of the Philosophy of the Upanishads

1. Origins of the Upanishads

IKEDA: In the fifth or sixth century BC, the Upanishads introduced into Indian Philosophy a strain of investigation which had been wanting in the Vedic period. Whereas in the Vedic period, religion had concentrated on sacrifice and prayers for the sake of prosperity and good fortune, in the time of the Upanishads attention was devoted to investigating the basic nature of man and the fundamental origins of the universe. I am interested in knowing why this switch to speculative thought occurred at this time and what prompted it.

KARAN SINGH: The Upanishads are known by the term *Vedanta*, which means both that, chronologically they come towards the end of the Vedas, and also that they represent the philosopical essence of the Vedas. We must always remember, however, that the Upanishads are a natural and integral culmination of the Vedas and do not represent a sharp divergence. Many of the ideas and concepts so brilliantly developed in the Upanishads can be traced directly to the early Vedas. For example, the extraordinary Hymn of Creation in the Rig Veda (X–129–1/7) is a philosophical statement that ranks with the most sublime religious literature of the world. It would, therefore, be incorrect to say that the Vedas concentrated solely on sacrifice and prayer for the sake of prosperity and good fortune. Indeed, as Sri Aurobindo has pointed out in his highly intuitive commentaries on the Vedas, all the great concepts that have dominated Hindu thought from the beginning are found there, though they are often so concealed under a wealth of symbolism that the meaning is clear only to the initiated.

What the Upanishads did was to express these concepts in intellectual terms.

IKEDA: Naturally, their origins are to be found in the Vedas; nonetheless, the Upanishads represent a great a leap forward. In attempting to explain the alterations, materialists have claimed that growth in productive power and the emergence of a non-producing class are essential to spiritual advance. When productivity is low, everyone is too desperately concerned with basic survival to indulge in metaphysical speculation. Perhaps one of the causes of the birth of Upanishadic philosophy was a revolution in agricultural techniques and a consequent increase in productivity. But material abundance does not invariably inspire speculative philosophy; at least as far as can be judged from circumstances in Japan today, affluence has stimulated no flood of sophisticated philosophical thinking.

At about the time of the origin of the Upanishads, Socrates and Plato were thinking and writing among the Greeks, another Aryan race. This might indicate that all Aryan peoples have a bent for metaphysical philosophy. But it does not explain why. Some historians claim that the Aryans originally came from the southern Caucasus; others insist that their homeland must have been northern Europe. There seems to be no way of knowing for certain which is correct. No matter where they lived, however, certain traits must have developed as a result of the environment—and ways of thinking and social forms which resulted from adjustment to it. Furthermore, since they had probably lived in their original homelands for tens of thousands of years and moved to the Indian and Balkan peninsulas only some three thousand years ago, the characteristics evolved in the original environment must have been stronger than any which developed later. Thus, though the presence of the right , conditions and the right ways of thinking account for the shift from Vedic to Upanishadic thought in Indian religious philosophy, the conditions under which those basic attitudes evolved and the stimulus that brought them to flower are not known. It is not clear whether this philosophical development was totally, independently Indian or whether outside influence came into play. Perhaps there can be no definite answers to these questions; nonetheless, I should very much like to hear your opinions on them.

KARAN SINGH: Whereas the Vedas were the spontaneous outpourings of the mystic vision of numerous seers and sages, the Upanishads present the teaching in a more structured and intellectually coherent manner. You are quite right in pointing out the interesting parallels between the Upanishads and the Socratic dialogues, which struck me forcefully when I first read these masterwords three decades ago. The introduction in the Upanishads of the dialogue form through which the teacher imparts the sublime knowledge to the student, obliges him to present the teaching in a phraseology and idiom that can be readily understood. For this reason the Upanishadic dialogues have emerged as one of the high watermarks of man's spiritual quest.

I would agree that the Aryan people are particularly prone to metaphysical philosophy. Certainly climatic, social and economic conditions must have had some influence; but I would suggest that the key to your question could lie in the possibility, under certain conditions, for normal waking consciousness to be replaced by a totally different level of mystical awareness. The seers of the Vedas had experienced such blissful states of consciousness and had developed a complex system of Yoga—including physical, moral, mental and spiritual disciplines, that are conducive towards such transcendental experiences. It is well established that certain places are particularly favourable for the advent of the higher consciousness—mountain tops, river banks, and forest glades—and it is not without significance that, whereas the Socratic dialogues took place in the crowded city of Athens, the Upanishadic teachings are invariably set in quiet sylvan surroundings. Perhaps the basic difference between the Hindus and the Greeks is to be found here, which continues till today as a sort of watershed between eastern and western philosophy. Whereas, for the Greeks, brilliant intellectual speculation seems to have been an end in itself, in the Upanishads, however eloquent and impressive the words used, the mystical experience was always clearly beyond verbalization. Indeed in the Taittiriya Upanishad there is a famous sentence saying that the mystical level is one 'where words fall back along with the mind, unable to attain', meaning that intellectual activity alone cannot bring about the modification of consciousness that is the goal of the Hindu spiritual tradition.

IKEDA: In connection with the coeval metaphysical speculations of the ancient Aryans and Greeks, I am reminded of what the German philosopher Karl Jaspers says about pivotal periods in his *Vom Ursprung und Zeit der Geschichte* (Origins and Goals of History). He defines pivotal periods as times in which peoples attempt to plumb human nature and establish limitations and paramount goals. He set this pivotal period as the six centuries roughly between 800 and 200 BC, with a central point at about 500 BC, and saw this as a decisive dividing line in human psychological development. This time was of pivotal importance in the history of humanity because during it were produced the basic categories of thought and speculation and the beginnings of world religion on the basis of which we continue to live and think today.

According to one interpretation, individual personal names have been handed down in connection with various philosophical expressions in the Upanishads. Therefore, it is argued, the Upanishads represent recognition of the importance and significance of independent, individual philosophical speculation. This too may be intimately related to discovery of the human being as a trend of Jaspers' pivotal period.

2. *Teacher and Pupil in the Upanishads*

IKEDA: 'Upanishad' means a session in which a pupil is seated at the feet of a master, who imparts teachings. In the western, especially the Greek, interpretation of philosophy, teacher and pupil together engage in a dialogue oriented towards the discovery of truth. If my understanding of the situation is correct, the Upanishadic tradition is much more doctrinaire than this. Whereas, in the eyes of philosophy—love of knowledge—pupil and master are ultimately equal, the Upanishadic system seems to assume that the teacher has already attained knowledge which he then imparts to his pupil. Is this the case? Or does the Upanishadic teacher merely attempt to impart to his pupil a practical method by means of which wisdom and enlightenment to truth may be reached?

KARAN SINGH: The word 'Upanishad' has two meanings, which is not uncommon in Sanskrit where several shades of meaning can emerge from a single world. One meaning is that of a dialogue in which pupils sit around the teacher. But there is a second meaning related to the nature of the teaching, and this implies 'secret knowledge.' In the Upanishads, the teacher is expected to have two essential qualities; he must be *shrotriyam*, which means intellectually learned; and he must also be *brahmanishtham*, rooted in the experience of the Brahman. In other words, it is not enough for a teacher to be intellectually advanced, he must also be a person of spiritual attainment. Once this is understood, the reply to your question becomes clear. The teacher must impart both the intellectual knowledge and spiritual vision to students. If he has not achieved that knowledge himself, he obviously cannot teach it to his disciples, and if they already have the knowledge they obviously need no teacher. There was, therefore, no question of the pupils being equal to the teacher.

This explains the tremendous reverence in Hindu philosophy for the *Guru*. The word guru literally means the dispeller of darkness; and, by his spiritual power and intellectual ability, the teacher is expected to dispel the darkness of ignorance from the minds of his pupils. The reverence of the pupils for the teacher was reciprocated in the great affection and tenderness that gurus displayed towards their disciples, who are invariably referred to as *saumya*, a term of endearment and love.

IKEDA: In other words, the guru, who must be shrotriyam in connection with intellectual learning and brahmanishtham in terms of spiritual attainment, is the embodiment of both the religious thinker and the philosopher. As was often demonstrated by the ancient Greeks, essentially religion and philosophy are one. It was not until much more modern times in Europe that the two came to be separated. Nietzsche pointed out the limitations of the way of thinking involved in this split and warned of the debilitating effect it has on human life.

Today, this separation has reached an extreme and extends to all fields of a civilization in which a specialist in one discipline may be totally ignorant of a field of endeavour proximal to his own. But people are now coming to see that such specialization makes it difficult to see the totality of humanity and leads to a state of affairs devoid of a warm awareness of life. Our times are eagerly awaiting a restoration of human values on the basis of an understanding of the totality including human and all other forms of life. Re-examining the origins of Indian and other philosophies of the pivotal period can be most significant in efforts to attain such understanding.

3. Brahman and Atman

IKEDA: The oneness of *Brahman* and *Atman* is considered a fundamental tenet of the Upanishadic philosophy. Originally meaning a prayer or incantation, the word Brahman came to stand for holy knowledge or the great ubiquitous universal spirit that created all things and to which all things must return. Atman on the other hand, originally standing for *breath*, came to mean the essential self, or the self as opposed to all nonself, or other. In short, the Atman is the innermost, fundamental self after the outer physical covering of flesh has been stripped away and even the psychological self, represented by such things as will, thought, consciousness and desire, has been eliminated. The semantic change in the meanings of these words from actual actions and phenomena to profound, abstract concepts indicates a shift in human interest from superficial everyday affairs to transcendental basics. The concepts of Brahman and Atman evolved as an outcome of this process of philosophical thought, and show ancient Indian philosophy to have been more creative than anything seen in the early periods of western religions.

Other peoples have arrived at the formulation of a god-the-creator, the source of all things, that could be compared with Brahman. The religion of the Jews, the trunk from which sprang both Christianity and Islam, illustrates my point. But such religions have emphasized the power of the creator and have interpreted humanity as puny and helpless in the face of the divine: mankind is no more than one of God's many creations. When human beings turn their back on Him and transgress His code of laws, for example in the story of Noah, God retaliates by destroying all of them except for one family which does as He tells them. Ironically, though all human beings alive today are theoretically descendants of Noah's good family, the moral degradation in our world probably outstrips anything known to the human beings whom the Judaic God saw fit to destroy in the flood. Be that as it may, the point is that, though God's creatures, men are always prone to depravity and can be totally wiped out at God's whim. I suspect a teaching which makes humanity so triflingly unimportant.

Brahman is not an anthropomorphic god, but a principle. And the Atman existing within each human being is one with Brahman. Human beings possessing a core identifiable with the universal spirit are a far cry from human beings who can be totally anihilated by the will of a god.

KARAN SINGH: You have correctly appreciated the importance of the twin concepts of Brahman and Atman in the Hindu tradition, and your comments in this regard are very perceptive. There is indeed a fundamental difference between the concept of the Atman and the Semitic concept of God as an all powerful human figure sitting in the sky and, from his elevated position, issuing dictates that can be transgressed by man only at the risk of immediate destruction or permanent damnation. The great genius of the Hindu tradition lies in the concept of the divine power that pervades every atom of the universe, visible and invisible, manifest and unmanifest. The reflection of this divine power in the individual human being is the Atman, and the ultimate goal is the unity of the Atman with the Brahman, which leads to spiritual illumination. The process is known as Yoga, which comes from the same root as the English word *yoke* and implies the union of Atman and Brahman.

The Atman-Brahman concept is at the pole opposite to the Semitic concept of a God 'up there'. In Hinduism, the divinity is, in the ultimate analysis, seated *within* each individual. The concept of the Atman endows evey human individual with a spiritual dignity and stature cutting across all barriers of caste or class, religion or nationality. You are correct in pointing out that this concept powerfully upholds the inalienable dignity of the individual human being, particularly at a time when human dignity is at a discount and various collectivities seek to impose domination over the individual in a hundred ways.

4. The Four Stages of Human Life

IKEDA: I have heard that, in ancient India, old people retired to lead lives devoted to the attainment of a state of spiritual power and wisdom and union with Brahma. This practice was no doubt limited to the Brahman class, but the idea of coming to grips with the ultimate aspects of life without being obsessed by the pursuit of material wealth or sensual pleasure has much to teach people today. Ancient Indian thought divided human life into four stages, or *ashramas*, each of which, according to one explanation, lasted about twenty years. The first was that of Veda studentship, or *bramacharin*. During it, while studying with a guru, the young man was supposed to attain the qualities of respectfulness, diligence and faithfulness. The second stage was that of the householder, or *grhastha*. During it a man married, raised children, worked as the head of the house and did his duties in the eyes of society. During the third stage, the man entrusted his household and social duties to his grown sons and, with his wife, retired to a secluded forest to live the life of a hermit, or *vanaprastha*. And, in the fourth and last stage, he left all his possessions and his wife to live as a mendicant wanderer or *sanyasin*.

This, the ideal system, was doubtless beyond most men. First of all, it required eighty years, an age to which not many could hope to live. Apart from age, however, various other conditions and necessities stood in the way of abiding completely by this scheme. In poor homes, children had to help provide and could not afford to go and live with a guru for a period of twenty years. Not all married couples had sons to whom they could abandon their duties, and not all were able to go to live in hermit huts in the forest. (Even if they went, who would support them? Did their children remain concerned about their welfare?)

Again, I strongly doubt whether an old man could, or even ethically should, be cold-hearted enough to abandon an old, possibly sick, or dying, wife in the forests to go and live as mendicant.

The Upanishadic division of life into these stages is certainly not without importance (though probably practicable only for the Brahman caste, the hermit's life admirably avoided ensnarement in the pursuit of the wealth and pleasures of this world and thus, as I have said, has a significant message for mankind today) but it seems more realistic to approach the divisions not as mutually exclusive, one-time periods in life but as aspects of life that progress coevally until death. For instance, study is something that should continue throughout a human's lifetime. Though domestic and social duties too persist until the end, a man must not allow himself to become so engrossed in them that he neglects objective, philosophical inquiry into the nature of humanity and life. The kind of pursuit of faith and ultimate truth that the hermit and ascetic wanderer might be expected to engage in is essential to the spiritual growth and development of all human beings but must not be removed from the actual affairs of everyday life. (I am convinced that the hermit cannot reach ultimate truth precisely because he removes himself from general human affairs.)

Though I have these reservations about the system, I realize that it has been important to the Indians of the past and that it remains important for many Indians today.

KARAN SINGH: The division of human life into four stages, or ashramas, was indeed the ideal accepted by early Hindu society, although it probably remained only an ideal for all except a small number of people. Before I comment upon it, I must point out that each ashrama consisted of twenty-five not twenty years, which would raise the full lifespan of man to a round hundred. Indeed there are hymns in the Vedas praying for long life and health up to a hundred years.

It seems to me that the formalization of the four ashramas were a later development in Vedic life. The importance of the division, however, was clear from the very beginning. The student life was obviously essential and, given the complexity of Sanskrit and the broad spectrum of knowledge that had to be imparted, would require at least fourteen years of study with a guru. Assuming the child went to the guru at the age of about ten, this would bring him to about twenty-five years when he finished his education. Then came the grhastha, or household phase, during which young men were expected to marry, become productive members of society, and raise a family. The third, vanaprastha, stage was when the children had grown to maturity and the householder was expected gradually to release his grip over material possessions and to prepare for the great passing on. The sanyasa phase too was well-established, although, interestingly, was not dependent on any age. It was possible for people to renounce the world at any point in their lives if they felt the inner compulsion to do so, and this remains true in Hindu society today.

In the classical ashrama division, however, sanyasa came at a ripe old age after the children were all settled and the grandchildren too had come of age. Then the individual was freed from social responsibility and could take the final plunge into renunciation. And, if his wife were still alive, the children and grandchildren were expected to take good care of her; thus the question of abandonment did not arise. We must remember that the whole Hindu social order was based upon joint families that provided continuing economic and physiological support to all members of the family, regardless of age or occupation. The ashrama system seems to have been conceived as a broad structure to ensure that Hindu society retained its dynamism and that there was constant renewal and change of leadership. In contrast to the gerontocracy prevalent in some other societies, the ashrama system encouraged elderly people to move on in a graceful and socially acceptable manner and facilitated a natural renewal of leadership.

5. Upanishadic Philosophy and Buddhism

IKEDA: Since Buddhism grew in a spiritual environment pioneered by Upanishadic philosophy, the large number of similarities between the two is scarcely surprising. Although Hinayanists have sometimes claimed that the two are entirely different, true Buddhism never assumes so narrow a viewpoint. For instance, Nichiren Daishonin said that Brahmanism contains part of the truth: even before the advent of the Buddha some Brahmans in India came to the correct view of life through the Vedas. In addition, he said that Brahman thought provides grounds for an understanding of Buddhism. And the final conclusions of these non-Buddhist teachings constitute an important means of entry into Buddhism.

Nonetheless, since Buddhism is born of an awareness of the limitations of Upanishadic thought, the two are different in important ways. First, whereas Upanishadic philosophy is metaphysical and speculative, Buddhism concentrates on the practical issue of overcoming suffering in human life.

Gautama Buddha lived in seclusion and meditation for the period leading to his enlightenment. After this, however, he moved out among the ordinary suffering people and taught them the Law in order to encourage and enhearten them. His teachings were so simple that even the illiterate could understand them and put them to practical use in daily life.

The Upanishadic philosophy was for Gautama Buddha only part of his much larger enlightenment. Whereas, for the Upanishadic philosopher, truth was an external goal, for Gautama Buddha it was something which human beings could find within themselves. He therefore concerned himself with developing in human beings the wisdom requisite to such enlightenment and strove to enable people to find a broader, more truly happy way of living. This seems to me to explain why, though the Upanishadic philosophy never became part of the way of thinking of the ordinary masses, Buddhism transcended the caste system and all similar barriers to find acceptance among peoples from all classes.

KARAN SINGH: It is right to emphasize the fact that Buddhism grew in the spiritual environment pioneered by Upanishadic philosophy.

I agree that for the Buddha mere theoretical knowledge of possible enlightenment was insufficient. He was imbued with a tremendous inner compulsion to spread the message of enlightenment to the masses, and that is why he will always be revered in history as one of the great teachers of all time. As I see it, the basic difference between him and the seers of the Upanishads lies in the fact that, while the latter sought only to lead their direct pupils to enlightenment, the Buddha sought enlightenment for all mankind. This explains the widespread nature of the response that his teachings received. Another related reason, as you mention, was that he propounded his teachings in simple language that could be understood by the common masses irrespective of class and caste distinctions. Their chaste Sanskrit confined the Upanishads largely to the educated upper castes, although through the later Puranas the Vedantic teachings were popularized in a form readily assimilable by society at large.

IKEDA: The content and nature of the enlightenment that the Buddha experienced are deeply connected with his use of language easily understood by people of all castes and classes. As is concisely expressed in the explanation of the true nature of all phenomena in the Lotus Sutra, Gautama Buddha's enlightenment resulted from observation of the things that confront all human beings. This is clearly revealed in Chapter Five, 'The Way Leading to Nirvana', in the Suttanipatta, one of the oldest of Buddhist scriptures, in which Gautama Buddha's immediate disciples call him incomparable among all beings and say that he pointed out to those who listened the absence of delusion in all those phenomena that take no time and that are apparent to the eyes of anyone.

In many of his writings, Nichiren Daishonin, too, mentioned those things which are perfectly evident but that seem be insignificant, such as an eyelash or even emptiness.

Gautama Buddha taught in order to enlighten people to a truth that was so close at hand that it could be easily overlooked. In contrast to the Upanishadic philosophy, which thought of the truth of enlightenment as a goal to strive to attain, Buddhism has cultivated in human beings the wisdom to find enlightenment to the truth within themselves.

6. Goals of Buddhist and Upanishadic Thought

IKEDA: I should like to further pursue the differentiation between Buddhist and Upanishadic thought by looking at the goals of the two systems. For the attainment of the ultimate goal of union between Atman and Brahman, Upanishadic philosophy teaches the nonexistence and unimportance of all other things. Even though this might be true, totally ignoring everything in life but these two elements is difficult or impossible for all but a very limited number of people.

KARAN SINGH: The interactions between the Upanishadic and the Buddhist philosophies are extremely interesting, and need much closer study than they have received so far. In my view, it would be incorrect to say that the Upanishadic philosophy teaches the nonexistence and unimportance of all things other than Atman and Brahman. Perhaps you are referring to the celebrated doctrine of *Maya* in Hindu thought, which has caused a good deal of confusion among scholars. Maya certainly does not mean nonexistence. In fact it stands for the lower or lesser knowledge that ascribes to the manifold manifestations of the Universe an identity and distinctiveness apart from and independent of the one true reality, which is Brahman. Later in some schools of Hindu thought, Maya itself becomes the feminine principle and is worshipped as the Goddess through whose grace alone the veil of *avidya*, or ignorance, can be removed and the truth realized.

Because the Upanishads see the Brahman as permeating everything that exists, they reject the concept of nonexistence. Moreover, the Upanishads and, later, the Bhagavadgita, which is considered to represent the quintessence of Upanishadic wisdom, stress the importance of work in the world as a means of spiritual growth equal to, if not more effective than, renunciation. Whereas the Upanishadic philosophy accepts the possibility of realization even without external renunciation, my understanding of the Buddhist tradition is that only those who become members of the Sangha by renouncing their worldly ties can hope to achieve Nirvana. If this interpretation is correct, it would tend to support the view that the Upanishadic philosophy is more life-affirmative.

IKEDA: Gautama Buddha himself had lived as a hermit and he explained ascetic discipline to others in his early teachings. But later Mahayana Buddhism put little value on asceticism. It is true that Mahayanists departed from the ordinary way of life to become monks and devote themselves to study and training. They did not, however, adopt this course solely for the sake of their own discipline, but in order to fulfil, after completing their study, the duty of taking the Buddhist teachings to as many people as possible. In other words, instead of acting solely for personal upliftment, the Mahayana Buddhist priest was motivated by the altruistic desire to benefit all society.

Instead of eliminating everything but one's own supreme core (in Upanishadic terms, the Atman), the Buddhist way is to recognize other entities and make use of them as guides along the way to the attainment of the ultimate Self (Atman). It is therefore necessary to elucidate the principles on which this is to be done. In my opinion, among all Buddhist scriptures, the Lotus Sutra is the one that explains them most clearly.

The Lotus Sutra teaches that all objects and life forms—in other words, all phenomena—are essentially the same as the one universal entity. It is less than completely objective to describe as nonexistent those elements of will, desire, thought and consciousness that play a part in the daily lives of all of us. Indeed most of us cannot live without becoming engrossed in these aspects of life.

On the basis of the principle that all phenomena are essentially the same as ultimate truth, Buddhism teaches how the will, desires, thoughts and consciousness—*klesha* or pain-producing delusions—arising in daily life may be converted into a way to total wisdom (enlightenment) or *bodhi*. To know the nature of the ultimate, it is necessary to eliminate the delusions concealing it. The Lotus Sutra approach, however, is to keep one's eye fixed on the ultimate, while enjoying and making use of phenomena experienced along the way.

The person who is constantly and totally absorbed in the ultimate might be compared to someone lost in a forest and earnestly seeking the way he must follow. Every tree or blade of grass is an obstacle for him. The Buddhist in the same forest already knows the way he must follow and, experiencing no distress, is able to feel at home with the trees and the grasses as he strolls about happily making various discoveries. In other words, the teachings of the Lotus Sutra instruct the believer in the way to the attainment of ultimate truth while allowing him to lead an ordinary existence, and to employ the consciousness, desires and thoughts he constantly encounters to invigorate and enrich his life.

KARAN SINGH: The point you make relating to the elimination of delusions is an important one. To take up your parable of the man lost in the forest, in the Upanishadic teachings, if he were to achieve spiritual realization he would have no need to get out of the forest at all, as the forest itself would for him become the abode of Brahman. I would once again stress a point I made earlier: the enlightenment of the Upanishads represents a qualitative change of consciousness; and, once that is achieved, the outer circumstances of life are no longer of cardinal importance. In the process of enlightenment, of course, in the Upanishadic as well as the Buddhist tradition, both the painful and pleasurable circumstances of life can be used as positive factors for spiritual growth.

7. Origins of the Idea of Transmigration

IKEDA: Though the idea of transmigration is thought to have been formulated originally in the Upanishads, it is interesting to note that it is not exclusively Indian, since Pythagoras too believed in it. Indeed, the English word *metempsychosis*, which means transmigration as Pythagoras understood it, is of Greek derivation. The famous story of his having upbraided a friend for kicking a dog because it might actually be the body housing the soul of the friend's deceased father suggests that perhaps for many Greeks of his day the idea was not totally far-fetched.

Of course, similarities between things Greek and things Indian are not surprising. Both Sanskrit and Greek belong to the same Indo-Aryan family. Fustel de Coulanges, in his book *La Cite Antique*, quotes extensively from the Lawbook of Manu in an analytical presentation revealing many similarities of thought and life-style between the people of Greece and those of India and comes to the conclusion that both societies rested on a common ideology. This leads me to suspect that the idea of transmigration is a part of a larger Indo-Aryan way of thinking that pre-dates even the Upanishads.

The idea may have been unformulated and taken for granted until the Upanishadic delving into the nature of the Atman necessitated its clarification. If we assume great antiquity for the idea that good acts in this life ensure rebirth in fortunate circumstances of mind, appearance and health in the next, and that evil acts condemn their perpetrator to rebirth in an unfortunate state, we can see that it was the achievement of the Upanishads to add to this idea the notion of a constant core capable of migrating from one life to another, and to identify this core as the Atman. To pin down and examine the intangible, invisible Atman required a high level of abstract speculative ability.

I think—though it is no more than a personal opinion for which I lack documentary or other substantiation—that positing a changeless core or Atman led to the awareness that all entities are fundamentally equal. But it then became important to explain the apparent inequalities that set entities apart from each other in our actual experience. To explain this, I believe the ancient Indian philosophers turned back to the very old idea of transmigration and *karma*. What is your evaluation of my opinion?

KARAN SINGH: It is true that the idea of transmigration is found in many of the world's great religions. Even in the Semitic religions there is a belief in the survival of the soul after death, but they posit only a single life after which the soul will wait in limbo for aeons before final judgement. In the Eastern religions, however, the concept of rebirth is central to the entire philosophy, and closely linked with this is the concept of karma.

It is very important that the concept of karma be understood correctly. Some western thinkers have mistakenly argued that karma simply means a fatalistic acceptance of the human situation. In fact the contrary is true. Karma implies that at any given point of time, each individual has the capacity, and indeed must be aware of the necessity, to choose between various alternative modes of action, and based upon this choice, will reap the effects of that action. 'Good' actions assist in release from ignorance and passion, while 'evil' actions cause the person to get furher bogged down in these attitudes and thus make eventual release more difficult. It is the genius of the Upanishads to be able to combine the concept of the undying Atman with that of karma, and thereby create a framework for moral and spiritual development of the individual human being.

Clearly, the concepts of transmigration and karma are closely linked, but whether the awareness of the Atman preceded the concept of karma is difficult to postulate. It would seem to me that, once the seers of the Upanishads had direct experience of the immortal Atman, the development of a detailed theory of karma became an intellectual necessity not only to explain the actual state of inequality that existed around them, but also to lay before human beings a clear path of action that would ultimately lead to enlightenment. The Buddhist attitude seems to be very similar to this.

8. The Desirability—or Undesirability—of Being Born Again

IKEDA: As we have already mentioned, the ancient Indians believed in the doctrine of transmigration, according to which the dead human being is born again into this world. The ancient Egyptians too believed that the dead could return to the world of the living. Indeed, they considered such rebirth so important that they went to elaborate ends to mummify and preserve corpses and, when funds were available, as they were in the cases of the pharaohs, erected huge monuments as houses for the dead. The ancient Indians, on the other hand, considered transmigration—a concept originating in the Upanishads and not found in the old Vedas—so distasteful that great thinkers strove to devise ways of escaping from its endless, or at any rate very long, cycles. The Upanishads set forth two fates for the life which persisted after death. After cremation, the persisting life could travel the way of light and go to dwell in immortality in the moon: this was the way of the gods, and most desirable. The less desirable fate for the persisting life would be to fall again to earth as rain and re-enter the cycle of birth, life, death and rebirth.

Why should the two peoples have taken such different views of this issue? Life cannot have been all joy and pleasure for any Egyptian, even a pharaoh. On the other, it cannot have been total misery for all ancient Indians, for whom technical advances had made living easier and who took delight in music, dancing and literature. Still the ancient Egyptian wanted to come back, and the ancient Indian did not. My own personal interpretation of this difference is related to climate and weather.

The highest god for the Egyptians was the sun. The sun is always in this world; therefore, the ancient Egyptians could conceive of no happiness away from the sun and the world it governs. Indra was the most widely worshipped of the Indian gods, probably because he is associated with thunder, the harbinger of the rains that are essential to life in the Indian subcontinent. The alternation of wet and dry seasons in India may have suggested the inconstancy and endless transmutation of all natural phenomena. In contrast with this inconstant world, the Indians probably posited a changeless world where immutable happiness was to be found. They naturally longed to find their way out of the cycles of transmigration and into this happy realm of constancy.

KARAN SINGH: One of the most striking differences between the Egyptian and the Indian approaches to death, as you have rightly pointed out, lies in their attitude towards the body. Whereas the ancient Egyptians seemed to have had an almost morbid obsession with the visible form of man even after death, in India from the time of the Vedas the Hindus have always believed that the body is mortal and must ultimately return to ashes. To me this seems a much healthier and more enlightened attitude and has nothing to do with the texture of life on earth. Burning the corpse not only was an effective method of preventing the spread of disease and epidemics, but was also psychologically satisfying. The sacred fire of Vedic times was always looked upon with great veneration; Hindu weddings are performed by circumambulating fire, and the entire Vedic ritual of the *Yagna* was based upon oblations to fire. The cremation of the body, and the subsequent immersion of the ashes in the Ganga or some other sacred river, provide a clean and satisfying end to physical existence. This has nothing to do with Indra or any of the other Vedic Gods.

The point as to whether rebirth was sought or avoided because life on earth was pleasant or unpleasant is one that lies at the root of most of the religious traditions of the world. Buddhism in particular, with its constant emphasis on life as suffering (*dukha*), seems to be very prone to the conclusion that rebirth must be avoided. But, even if life were full of material and physical pleasure, the three inescapable elements of illness, old age and death are the lot of every person born into this world. The Upanishads postulate release from the round of births and deaths by ascending to a plane transcending both these dualities.

IKEDA: This plane is Nirvana, or release from the cycle of transmigration, and total extinction. Hinayana Buddhism sought Nirvana through the destruction of life. Nirvana is taught by Mahayanists, too, but in a different sense.

Mahayana Buddhism subscribes to the idea that human beings cannot escape from the cycle of life, death and rebirth, but it sees a constant, greater life behind all transient phenomena. Enlightenment to this greater life leads to Nirvana, which in this interpretation is a state of changeless bliss. In other words, the Mahayanist interpretation runs counter to the original meaning of the word Nirvana (extinction) to signify something that is eternal and incapable of extinction. In the light of my own awarness of the nature of life, the Mahayanist explanation is more convincing because it illustrates the dual nature of ceaseless alteration on a ground of persisting constancy that we all experience in our own lives. For instance, while realizing that I am constantly changing physically and psychologically, I nonetheless perceive a substratum of self that has remained constant since childhood.

Perhaps the individual, actual life of the present should be discussed on a level different from that required for an examination of transmigration beyond the life and death of the individual. But studying the two together in this way seems to shed revealing light on both.

KARAN SINGH: The concept of Nirvana in Buddhism is paralleled by the concept of release (*Moksha*) in Hinduism. If looked upon as total extinction, Nirvana would be a negative and unsatisfactory concept because it would reduce this entire glorious universe to a terrible mistake that should never have occurred. The more positive view of Mahayana Buddhism, which looks upon Nirvana as enlightenment leading to a state of changeless bliss (*ananda*), is much more satisfying and closer to the Upanishadic ideal. Nirvana indeed can be looked upon as the extinction of the false ego and the completion of the process of self-enlightenment.

The exact processes whereby Nirvana is achieved are not easy to describe. Clearly the act of dying in itself is insufficient, because, although the material body perishes, the Atman continues its evolution in a subtle body returning again and again to human birth until final release is obtained. It is important to remember that both Hinduism and Buddhism subscribe to the concept of enlightenment of a human being while still alive on this earth, and do not simply promise some heaven after death.

9. *Transition from the Mythical to the Philosophical*

IKEDA: Both Upanishadic philosophy and Buddhism are outstanding for the way they interpret human life as being one with the universe. And, if such an interpretation is valid, it would seem that all human beings in the universe should be equally deserving of respect. Nonetheless, the Indian caste system, which takes it origins in Hindu mythology born of Upanishadic philosophy, is a classic example of discrimination.

Vedic literature set forth the system of four classes (*varna*) that became a characteristic of Indian society. This literature explained that all things were born from a primeval man, Purusha, who was ritually divided into parts from which developed the four classes: the Brahmans came from his mouth, the ruling warrior class or Kshatriyas came from his arms, the mercantile class or Vaishyas came from his thighs, and the lowest class—the servile class, or Shudras—came from his feet. The same tradition is carried over into the Upanishads.

According to this myth, differentiations among individual beings are irrevocably fixed; and no human effort or will can do anything to alter them. In other words, human beings are compelled to remain in the class into which they are born. This in turn means that the dignity of souls resulting from oneness with the universal soul is impotent in the face of actual human inequalities.

The Buddhist view is different from this. According to Buddhist philosophy, life continues eternally and manifests itself in a series of transmigratory births and rebirths. The individual is responsible for his own characteristics and for any inequalities, since his acts, through the law of cause and effect, influence his karma that in turn determines the condition into which he will be born the next time. Though each individual life differs from all others, since all lives obey the One Universal Law, they are all essentially equal. Furthermore, the Buddhist approach demonstrates complete respect for the dignity of the individual by insisting that all sentient creatures have ability, through their actions, to influence their own fate.

The law of cause and effect rests on the assumption that all lives are preceded by an infinite number of former lives, that is, none were ever created or generated at a given point in the past.

Since the philosophical concepts of primal, eternal and infinite are difficult to grasp, all peoples have resorted to myths—like that of Purusha—to explain the drama of creation. The Upanishads seem to me to represent a transitional phase between the mythic stage and the truly philosophical stage later represented by the concepts of cause and effect and karma and the eternity of life as formulated in Buddhism. I should like to hear your interpretation of the current that connects the views on karma in the Upanishads with those in Buddhism, and your ideas on elements mediating between the mythic stage of the Vedas and philosophical Buddhist thought.

KARAN SINGH: The great myths of the Vedas can be interpreted on several different levels. At the most fundamental level, they offer deeply intuitive, symbolic representations of the origins of the solar system and indeed of the universe itself. Thus the great horse sacrifice mentioned in the Rig Veda shows the process of cosmo-genesis whereby the unmanifest supreme power, by a process of self-limitation, takes upon itself the burden of matter and blazes into manifestation. At another level, very much later in time, these myths represent the first beginnings of human civilization when man emerged from the chaos of the Stone Age to become human. Still later, they represent the progressive evolution of consciousness, and this is most clearly visible in the avatara myths of Hindu Pauranic literature, in which the manifestations of Vishnu clearly follow the evolutionary path from the ocean, where life first began, through amphibious, mammalian, semi-human, and then human forms.

It is important to keep in mind this aspect when dealing with a powerful myth like the origin of the four classes from the primeval Purusha. To take its meaning literally would be to miss the whole sweep of imagination that is such an important element of Vedic literature. In all societies, a broad division into the priestly, the warrior and the agricultural classes was quite common; and, if we add to them the absorption of indigenous people, we already have the embryonic fourfold caste system. In time, perhaps owing to the intellectual predominance of the priestly class, the varna system became a permanent part of Hindu society. It is important to remember, however, that, in the Bhagavadgita, Lord Krishna says that the fourfold varna system has been created on the basis of inner propensity and outer work. This would imply that it was not always looked upon as a rigid structure, although certain elements of rigidity did enter into the picture later.

I might recall that the first great Hindu empire was founded by Chandragupta Maurya, who was considered to be from a low caste, and many of the greatest saints and sages in Hindu history have come from the so-called lower castes. Consequently, while it could be looked upon as a method of socially organizing a vast population, the caste system never stood in the way of spiritual realization or emancipation. Many of the uncomplimentary references to Shudras could well be later interpolations rather than parts of the original text.

The caste system has been the cause of a great deal of confusion among non-Hindu commentators. Ideally it was supposed to provide a medium for spiritual growth to people belonging to different stages and propensities. All over the world, men can be divided into four great types: there is the Brahman, the teaching, priestly, legal or professional type; the Kshatriya, the ruler, warrior, statesman type; the Vaishya or banking, merchant, agricultural type; and lastly the Shudra the servant, manual labourer type. It should be noted that the qualities ideally possessed by the four castes are of a moral and intellectual nature. In this the Gita agrees with the Buddha, who also said 'not by naked hair, nor by lineage, nor by birth is one a Brahman. He is a Brahman in whom there are truth and righteousness.' (Dhammapada 3.9.3).

Before I end my comments on this point, I must introduce the concept of *Gunas*, which is important for an understanding of Hindu philosophy. The three Gunas—*Satva, Rajas,* and *Tamas*—could be translated as harmonious purity, passionate activity, and dark inertia, respectively. In the Hindu system, these three Gunas are involved in all manifestation, and the path of release or Moksha lies in moving from Tamas to Rajas, then advancing to Satva, and finally transcending the Gunas altogether. The ideal person in the Gita is described as *Gunatita*, one who has risen above the Gunas. In the caste system, the ideal Brahman, detatched and pure, seeing the one in all, stands for the Satvik guna; the Kshatriya, fearless and enduring, represents Rajas guna; the Vaishya, concerned with the generation of wealth, symbolizes the desire nature, Rajas mixed with Tamas, always flowing downwards; and the Shudra, born to serve, stands for the Tamasic, physical body, the instrument of all.

Even within a single human being the various organs of the body could be taken to represent this fourfold order. The head, which represents the intellectual faculty, corresponds to the Brahman element; the arms, which are the fighting organs, the Kshatriya element; the stomach, which involves the constant intake and circulation of food, to the Vaishya element; and the legs, which are constantly serving the body and upon which all the others rely, to the Shudra element.

The Buddha did not confine his teachings to any particular caste, and this was probably where he differed from the traditional teachers of the Upanishads. If no caste existed in the Sangha, however, there was none in the Hindu Sanyasi orders either. Once the saffron-coloured robe of a monastic order has been donned, the Hindu has shed his caste background and is no longer addressed by any caste appellation. Like the pure mountain air that blows among the pines, fertilizing all and yet attached to none, the realized being moves about amidst the throng of men. Whether he lives in a crowded city or on a lonely mountain peak, he is a Homeless One, for, though he may fulfil social duties, yet neither family nor caste, race nor religion, holds him in bondage.

CHAPTER THREE

Buddhism and Indian Society

1. Important Dates

IKEDA: There are various theories about the dates of the birth and death of Gautama Buddha, though the traditional belief, based on records in many Buddhist scriptures, that he lived for eighty years is fairly certainly correct. Of the many interpretations of the actual dates, three have found acceptance among Japanese Buddhists. According to a work entitled 'Gao-seng Faxian Chuan', concerning the famous Chinese priest and pilgrim to India, Faxian (who lived in the fourth century of the Christian Era), Gautama Buddha is thought to have died in 1087 BC.

Another theory is based on the tradition that a drop of some fragrant substance was put in the *Vinaya* annually by Gautama Buddha's disciples and their successors. It is believed that this practice originated with the disciple Upali at a council to codify the teachings shortly after the Buddha's death. In the fifth century, the Indian monk and scholar Samghabhadra travelled to Guangzhou, in China and, after translating the *Vinaya* into Chinese, put in a drop, bringing the total to 975 drops. It is known that Samghabhadra did this in AD 490. Back-reckoning from this date gives us 485 BC as the date of the Buddha's death.

The third of the traditionally accepted dates is based on a Chinese document called 'Zhou-shu-yi-ji', which claims that the Buddha was born on April eighth of the twenty-fourth year of the reign of King Zhao and that he died on February fifteenth of the fifty-second year of the reign of King Mu. On the basis of this information, the noted Chinese priest Falin, who was active in the Sui and Tang dynasties, fixed the date of Gautama Buddha's death as 949 BC. Chinese and Japanese Buddhists have favoured this dating.

While applying scientific principles of investigation and analysis to historical research, modern western Indianologists nonetheless differ on these important dates. They have established the date of the ascension of King Ashoka by referring to the date of Alexander the Great's invasion of India. Adding to this the Sri Lankan belief that King Ashoka ascended the throne either 218 or 219 years after Gautama Buddha's death, these scientists put the latter date at either 477 or 478 BC.

Starting from a different angle, other western scholars have dated Ashoka's accession to the throne on the basis of five foreign kings named in the edicts the Indian king caused to be engraved on rocks and pillars in various parts of India. From the known dates of these foreign kings, the scholars posit the ascension of Ashoka in either 270 or 271 BC. Using the Sri Lankan figure of 218 or 219 years between Gautama Buddha's death and King Ashoka's ascension they reckon back and reach a date of about 488 BC for the death of Gautama Buddha. According to some Indian traditions, however, Ashoka mounted the throne only 100 or 116 years after Gautama Buddha's death, which brings that event a century closer to us in time. In line with this and with recent scholary research moving the date of ascension of King Ashoka farther forward, Hajime Nakamura, professor emeritus at Tokyo University, claims that the date of Gautama Buddha's death should be set at 383 BC.

In 1956–7, Buddhists in India, Sri Lanka, Burma, Thailand, Laos and Cambodia celebrated the 2,500th anniversary of Gautama Buddha's death, which they must therefore place at 544 BC.

Further study and research may produce grounds for establishing one reliable system of dating Gautama Buddha's life. Or perhaps, like many other dates in ancient Indian history, these too will always remain uncertain. What are your opinions on the possibility of accurately establishing these dates? What are the opinions of modern Indian archaeologists and scholars on this subject?

KARAN SINGH: As you say, there has been a good deal of uncertainty and controversy regarding the exact date of the birth and passing away of the Buddha. I doubt if any useful purpose will be served by my going into the details of the various theories put forward in this regard, some of which you have mentioned in your remarks. Of the various scholars you mention, Professor Hajime Nakamura is well known to me personally and is a man of great erudition.

In May 1956, the 2500th anniversary of the *Mahaparinirvana* of the Buddha was celebrated throughout the world; and there was general acceptance of this date, although not every country agreed with it. The major celebrations in India, in which the eminent philosopher Dr S. Radhakrishnan, then vice-president of India, and Prime Minister Jawaharlal Nehru took a leading role, were held on the full-moon day of May 1956. According to this calculation, and accepting the tradition that the Buddha lived for a full eighty years, the date of his birth generally accepted in India would be 624 BC.

As a working hypothesis I would say that this date seems to be quite satisfactory until such time as further archaeological or other research can establish another date beyond any doubt. May I add, however, that the teachings of the Buddha are timeless and we need not be unduly obsessed with the actual dates involved. In the Hindu tradition, the *content* of a teaching is always considered to be more important than its chronology.

IKEDA: Essentially I agree that, from the standpoint of the believer, the content of a teaching and its power to relieve the suffering of people is of primary importance, and historically dating the origins of such teachings is of only secondary significance. But, from the historian's viewpoint, problems of this kind cannot be overlooked in examinations of the confluence of various religious ideas. I look forward to the time when greater accuracy about ancient Indian history in general will solve problems of this nature.

2. The Revolutionary Aspects of Buddhism

IKEDA: Buddhism (often, I understand, ranked as part of Hinduism in India today) was revolutionary in the India of Gautama Buddha's day for three reasons. First it taught that all human beings are equal under *Dharma*, or the Law, and, as has been mentioned, in this way criticized and rejected the Indian system of four classes. In a passage of the Lotus Sutra that you have already quoted, Gautama Buddha said that a person was not a Brahman or a non-Brahman by birth alone but by deeds. In other words, contrary to the tradition that a person born into a Brahman home was by virtue of heritage entitled to be considered an individual of great moral standing (in other words, a Brahman), Gautama Buddha said that birth was beside the point and that correct actions made a person a Brahman. (It should be pointed out that in this context the word *Brahman* refers, not to a member of a caste, but to a person of nobility of spirit.) Similarly, a person was not base merely because he was born into the Shudra class. Egalitarianism was strictly applied in the Order (Sangha), where all, no matter what their former wordly rank, were equal as disciples of the Buddha.

The second revolutionary aspect of Buddhism was its direct and persistent examination of the actualities of human life. Gautama Buddha interpreted the cycle of life—birth, aging, illness and death—as suffering, and he evolved a method for liberation from it. Other religions of the day posited the existence of supernatural creator spirits or supernatural powers, and by means of prayers, incantations, mystical practices and magical powers attempted to win the good graces of these forces. Gautama Buddha rejected and denied all this and insisted on concentrating on human realities. For this reason, western philosophers have referred to him as the first existentialist in history. In his method for escape from the suffering of life, Gautama Buddha relied on no transcendent gods, absolute powers or supernatural forces, but always taught that enlightenment to the Law existed deep within all human beings. He strove to awaken people to the great life force of constancy, joy, the true self and purification existing in the profoundest realms beyond the life of suffering. In his final words of advice, Gautama Buddha told his followers, 'Be lights unto yourselves. Rely on yourselves. Relying on no other persons, make the Law your guiding light and support. Rely on nothing else.' This wise counsel suggests that Buddhism may have been the fountainhead of oriental humanism.

The third revolutionary element is Buddhism's rejection of substantialism for the sake of a system of thought based on relativity as represented by the law of cause and effect.

These three revolutionary elements enabled Buddhism to spread beyond the limits of India and to find welcome among peoples throughout eastern and southeastern Asia and other parts of the world. In other words, these are the elements accounting for the universal nature of Buddhism.

KARAN SINGH: It is true that several elements of the Buddha's teachings were in marked contrast to patterns of thought existing among his contemporaries. The word *revolutionary* has several interpretations, but you are right when you say that the major departure of the Buddha was from the rigidities of the Hindu caste system, particularly from the claim that the Brahmans had a virtual monopoly over spiritual salvation. As I have pointed out in response to an earlier question, however, it must be remembered that, while caste distinctions were important in the Hindu social order, as far as philosophical and spiritual dimensions are concerned the Upanishads teach that all human beings are equal in the sense that the Atman in all of them is a manifestation of the Divine. The Buddha's egalitarian teachings were indeed a valuable and noble contribution; and in the later history of Hinduism, particularly with the advent of the great saint singers of the Bhakti movement in the medieval period, the revolt against rigid caste structures spread throughout the country.

With regard to your second point, it is true that the Buddha was deeply concerned with the actual sufferings of human beings and spread the gospel of service and compassion as a potent means not only of relieving suffering, but also of working out the individual's own karma. However, the concept of service to the suffering has always been embedded in the Hindu tradition, and the merit to be acquired by good deeds is accepted as being an important factor in spiritual development.

The major difference here would seem to revolve around the concept of the Atman. For the Buddha, his whole world-view stemmed from his First Noble Truth, the existence of suffering or dukha, which he looked upon as a fundamental feature of existence. In sharp contradistinction to this, the seers of the Upanishads looked upon all existence basically as ananda or bliss. It might be said that the Buddha's perception more accurately reflected the lot of the common man in India and, for that matter, in the rest of the world at that time; but there does seem to be an element of negativism in viewing human existence entirely from the viewpoint of suffering. In spite of the ocean of suffering in which they dwelt, the sages of the Upanishads postulated ananda rather than dukha as the inner core of human existence.

As far as the third point regarding substantialism is concerned, I see here the basic difference between the Hindu and Buddhist viewpoints. While the Buddha evidently rejected the doctrine that there are substantial realities behind external phenomena, Hinduism has always believed that physical phenomena are simply manifestations of a deep, undying, glowing reality—the Brahman. Which of these two doctrines is more 'revolutionary' is a matter of opinion, but it does seem to me that unless one accepts a deeper reality behind all existence, the whole cosmos is reduced to a ghastly mistake, which should never have occurred, and the glorious efflorescence of consciousness to what Bertrand Russell called 'a fortuitous conglomoration of atoms'.

IKEDA: I agree with you. The point is very difficult, but the

Buddhist explanation of what you call 'the deeper reality behind all existence' is roughly this. The Lotus Sutra teaches that all phenomena are one with essential reality and that all things come into being as a result of cause. At the same time, however, it holds that phenomena themselves are all manifestations of the Law, or the ultimate reality. In other words, instead of being 'fortuitous', all things are the majestical Law (Dharma).

3. The Flourishing Period of Buddhism in India

IKEDA: The development of Buddhism in India began in the central cultural region, known as the *Majjhima-janapada*, where Gautama Buddha himself taught, and then spread through other regions gradually to encompass most of India.

Centering around the Ganga, the *Majjhima-janapada* extends to Kuru-pancala in the northwest, and to Nalanda and Rajagaha, in what was then Magadha (modern Bihar) in the southeast. The Buddha himself did most of his teaching in such cities as Savatthi (capital of the kingdom of Kosala), Rajagaha (capital of the kingdom of Magadha), Vaishali (capital of the kingdom of Vaggi), Kapilavastu (capital of the state of the Shaka clan) and Kosambi (capital of the kingdom of Vansa). Of all of these, Savatthi and Rajagaha were the most important. During the same period, the Buddha's disciples took his teachings still farther to the southwest: to Avanti in the northern part of the Vindhya mountains and to the Sunaparatna district north of modern Bombay. The four or five centuries following the death of Gautama Buddha are the period of primitive and sectarian Buddhism. During this time, Buddhism spread to most parts of India and, especially during the reign of King Ashoka (third century BC), exerted its influence in all directions from the Indian subcontinent. At about the beginning of the Christian Era, it experienced a tremendous revival movement in the form of the emergence of Mahayana Buddhism. Thereafter, however, its fortunes in India declined.

KARAN SINGH: Perhaps the tremendous influence Buddhism has had on Indian history and culture ever since its advent, could be studied under four separate categories, the first of which is the impact upon the social structure. Quite clearly, the egalitarian social philosophy of Buddhism weakened the rigidities of the caste system in the areas of its influence and paved the way for the great upsurge of popular religious movements that persist to the present day. The Indian social structure was never to be the same after the advent of the Buddha, and although caste rigidities do continue to some extent even now, the Buddha's role in bringing about an egalitarian spirit was a major one.

The second impact is in terms of religious philosophy. While the *Anatmavad* (doctrine of non-atman) preached by the Buddha never took root in India, his teachings did have a valuable influence in several areas, specially that of animal sacrifice. In fact, after the Buddha, animal sacrifice, prevalent among many aboriginal tribes and castes of Hinduism, began to disappear, as indeed did the whole tradition of sacrificial rites, whether or not they involved animal sacrifice.

Thirdly, Buddhism has had a tremendous influence upon the art and culture of India. The first temples in Ajanta and Ellora were carved out of living rock by Buddhist monks, and the Gandhara influence upon Indian art remained a predominent motif for many centuries. Some of our greatest works of art, such as the Mathura Buddha of the Gupta period, the great stupa at Sanchi, the Bodh Gaya temples, and the Ajanta and Ellora caves, testify to this beneficient impact.

Lastly, Buddhism has had a major political influence, particularly through the great emperor Ashoka who spread the tenets of Buddhism far and wide in India and abroad. During his period, the noble message of the Buddha spread from India to neighbouring countries and began the long movement that ultimately took it to China and Japan. All in all, therefore, it can be said with confidence that Buddhism had an extremely beneficial influence upon Indian culture, and its role in Indian history will remain an important one.

4. Characteristics of Mahayana Buddhism

IKEDA: The issue of the difference between Mahayana and Hinayana cannot be overlooked in any discussion of the development of Buddhism. Of course, there was no such division during Gautama Buddha's lifetime. Nonetheless, Gautama Buddha always adjusted his method of teaching and the content of what he had to say to the abilities of his audience and to the occasion. And the resulting differences, which suggest the distinction between Mahayana and Hinayana, are the basis for the systematization of the sermons he delivered.

After Gautama Buddha's death, disagreement about the way the Order (Sangha) should be operated caused a split into the Theravadins and the Mahasamghika. The conservative Theravadins stressed observance of the monastic precepts, whereas the more liberal Mahasamghika put more emphasis on missionary work among the people. Since each held its own Second Council for the compilation of the sutras, the difference in emphasis that set the two apart is reflected in the scriptures themselves.

Thereafter the process of schism continued until there were eighteen or twenty different factions with various scriptures and training methods of their own. In the time of King Ashoka, the Third Council was held to compile scriptures and unify the various traditions handed down by the sects. But division continued and, under the repression of the Shunga dynasty, sectarian Buddhism was further weakened.

As this happened, believers in Mahayana teachings in various regions, fearing that if conditions persisted as they were Buddhism would perish entirely, decided to return to the basic teachings of Gautama Buddha and instigated a revival movement to reform Buddhism from within.

Although the Theravadins criticized the Mahayanists as

not being Buddhists at all, such outstanding people as Ashvaghosha (second century) and Nagarjuna (second or third century) believed in its teachings, though at first belonging to Hinayana organizations, and established the superiority of Mahayana.

Although they originated with the Mahayanists, the very designations Hinayana (Lesser Vehicle) and Mahayana (Greater Vehicle) suggest development from a state in which one is concerned solely with one's own enlightenment to a state in which the enlightenment of all sentient beings is a matter of the greatest importance. I suspect that the latter attitude more accurately reflects the Buddha's own approach.

KARAN SINGH: Every great teacher who speaks from spiritual enlightenment and not merely from the intellectual plane, expresses a broad spectrum of views on various matters, the emphasis differing according to the time and place the doctrine is preached. This is true of a great text like the Brihadaranyaka Upanishad, or of such teachers as Sri Krishna and Jesus Christ. Having preached over hundreds of square miles for half a century, the Buddha must inevitably, as you say, have adjusted his teachings to suit the place, the time and the audience. From the great reservoir of his wisdom, it would appear that specific schools have taken and developed different aspects of the teaching. As a Hindu, this does not surprise me. Indeed the multiplicity of philosophical and devotional sects within Hinduism flows precisely from this phenomenon. Whereas the semitic religions would tend to look upon such a development as a major schism—as, for example, that between the Roman Catholics and Protestants in Christianity, or the Shias and Sunnis in Islam—the Hindu tradition has been to respect and even welcome such plurality.

Your comment that the two major schools of Buddhism— Hinayana and Mahayana—began because the former laid emphasis on monastic precepts whereas the latter stressed missionary work is most interesting. To take a more recent example, Swami Vivekananda in our own century attempted to incorporate both these elements of Hinduism in two different but closely related organizations: the Ramakrishna Math is the monastic order, while the Ramakrishna Mission is enjoined with the task of spreading the gospel.

The fact that Buddhism spread to vast areas in India and to many countries abroad, each with differing linguistic, social, economic and cultural backgrounds, readily explains why Buddhism has developed into many sects over the last 2500 years.

IKEDA: In this connection, it is interesting to point out that, in contrast to the followers of the Semitic religions—Judaism, Christianity and Islam—who have slaughtered each other over the centuries, in spite of the existence of many sects, Buddhists have never engaged in large-scale religious warfare or resorted to great violence to prove their point.

KARAN SINGH: From the philosophic viewpoint, the major impact of Buddhism in the Indian tradition has been the emphasis on peace and non-violence, which was such an important element in Mahatma Gandhi's unique leadership of the Indian national movement. It is significant that our national flag bears the *Dharma Chakra*, which represents the wheel of the law in Buddhism, and that our national emblem itself is the lion capital of the Ashokan pillar at Sarnath, which rests upon this wheel. It is noteworthy that these have been adopted and accepted by a country which is eighty per cent Hindu and in which Buddhists represent hardly two per cent of the population. This clearly shows how important the Buddha's impact has been in India and is a fitting reply to those who charge that Buddhism has been banished from the country of its origin. It also highlights the unique capacity of Hinduism to accept and absorb the best from various traditions.

5. Kashmir and Buddhism's Way East

IKEDA: The importance of Kashmir, your own home, to Buddhism is very great.

Buddhism is said to have been introduced into Kashmir during the reign of King Ashoka. As is related in the works called, in Chinese, 'Shanjianlu-pipo-sha' (a commentary on the *Vinaya*) and in the 'Fufatsang-yinyuan-chuan' (which sets forth the lineage of priests in descent from Gautama Buddha), during the reign of King Ashoka a man named Madhyantika, said to have been the disciple of Ananda, one of the ten great disciples of the Buddha himself and therefore third in the direct descent of the Law, was dispatched to carry the Buddhist teachings to Kashmir. Chinese records make it clear that, as early as the first century BC, passage was possible from the city of Changan (modern Xian) through the Tarim basin, across the Kunlun Mountains, through Kashmir, and then to Gandhara and the city known at the time as Alexandria (either Ghazni or Kandhahar in modern Pakistan). In other words, in these remote times, Kashmir lay on the path that carried Buddhism from India to China and ultimately to Japan.

In the fourth and fifth centuries of the Christian Era, a series of priests of the highest worth and importance passed from India across the Kunlun range and then through the Taklamakan Desert to carry the teachings of the Buddha to China. For instance, in the final year (AD 381) of the reign of Fujian of the Earlier Chin dynasty, Samghabhadra came to the capital city of Ahangan, where he began work on translations of the Abhidharma-shastra and the Vasumitra-sutra and engaged in vigorous missionary work. His final fate is unknown. But this is not especially surprising since his life must have been very hard under the tumultuous political circumstances prevailing at the time.

Another great monk from Kashmir, Gautama Sam-ghadeva, came to Changan at about the same time and helped Samghabhadra work on the Vasumitra-sutra. Later he travelled to Loyang, where he worked on revisions of an existing translation of the Abidharma-shastra. Still later he crossed the Yangtse River and, in the region known as Jiangna, worked with Samgharasha, another monk from Kashmir, on a translation of the Madhyamagama-sutra. Samghabhadra's travels in China were extensive.

In the fifth century, Buddhayashas came to work in Changan. Born in Kashmir, at the age of thirteen he became a monk and is said to have memorized more than two million Hinayana and Mahayana sutras. Leaving Kashmir, he crossed Karakoram and went to what is now Kashgar, where he taught in the royal palace. At this time, the brilliant future scholar and translator Kumarajiva, who had been studying in Kashmir and was on his way home to Kucha, stopped to study with Buddhayashas. The further history of these two men is interesting and enlightening.

Upon returning to Kucha, his homeland, Kumarajiva found that it had been destroyed by a military expedition sent by Fujian of the Former Chin dynasty of China. He was himself taken prisoner and sent eastward to Changan, where he was greeted by the King Laoxing of the Latter Chin dynasty. Buddhayashas followed Kumarajiva, at whose request he was permitted to take part in the work of translating Buddhist texts then underway at Changan. He lent his assistance to Kumarajiva, who produced many outstanding translations. On Kumarajiva's death, however, Buddhayashas returned to Kashmir.

Among the other scholar-priests who travelled from Kashmir to China were Gunavarman (fifth-century translator) and Dharmamitra.

Both its location and the activities of many of its people have made Kashmir extremely important in Buddhism's eastward move.

KARAN SINGH: The Kashmir valley has always enjoyed a special position in India, not only because of its geographical location and exquisite natural beauty, but also because it has been the cradle of many great religious and spiritual movements from the very dawn of history. The Vedas were composed in the Himalayas, and surely Kashmir must have been among the places where the Vedic seers sang of the glory of Brahman and of the Divine Manifestation. A great Sanskrit work by Kalhana called *Rajatarangini* records the history of Kashmir over many centuries and is one of the few historical works in Sanskrit literature.

As you have pointed out, according to Chinese sources, Madhyantika, a disciple of Ananda, went to Kashmir and succeeded in bringing Buddhism there after having subdued indigenous Nagas through his supernatural powers. His visit to Kashmir is confirmed by Kashmiri sources, and it is believed that he brought many monks (*bhikshus*) with him to settle in Kashmir, where he remained himself for about twenty years.

The history of Kashmir is too complex to enter into even a brief description here. The Emperor Ashoka is believed to have sent missionaries to Kashmir, where according to persistent tradition, the fourth great international Buddhist Council was held, during the reign of Emperor Kanishka, in about AD 100 at a place called Harwan near Srinagar. Kashmir was for many centuries a centre of Buddhist learning both of the Mahayana and Hinayana schools. The greatest figure of Mahayana Buddhism, Nagarjuna, who is the progenitor of the Madhyamika school, is believed to have come either from the southern state of Andhra Pradesh or from Kashmir itself. Another great Sanskrit poet and Buddhist philosopher, Ashvaghosha, is believed to have belonged to Kashmir.

After the Hindu revival in the eighth century associated with the name of the great Hindu missionary Adi Shankaracharya, Buddhism in the Kashmir valley declined and gradually disappeared. It continues to flourish, however, in Ladakh to the present day. A large number of Buddhist monasteries, or *gumpas*, have been established there, many containing priceless manuscripts and works of art. Today Ladakh enjoys a special position within the Indian state of Jammu and Kashmir. One member, who is invariably a Buddhist, is elected from Ladakh to the Indian Parliament. In recent times the Head Lama of Spituk Monastery, Rimpoche

Kushak Bakula, and a representative of the old ruling family of Ladakh, Rani Parvati Devi, have represented the region in Parliament.

As this question refers to Kashmir, may I be permitted to add that the present state of Jammu and Kashmir was set up by my direct ancestor Maharaja Gulab Singh in 1846. My family always gave special consideration to the problems of the Buddhists in Ladakh, but it is interesting to recall that, in 1952, when my wife and I visited Ladakh where we were received with great enthusiasm and affection, it was the first time that a member of our immediate family had actually been there. As you rightly say, Kashmir constitutes an important cultural link between India and Japan. Of course Buddhism came to Japan not directly, but through China and Korea. Nonetheless, the sacred link remains, and I am happy that our dialogue is in some ways its revival and continuation.

6. Westward Influences

IKEDA: Recent research is showing that contacts and exchanges between ancient India and the western world were more numerous and frequent than might have been suspected. The oldest mutual influences were those related to trade between the Indus civilization and Mesopotamia. Later, various invasions—the Aryans, the Achaemenian Persians and the Macedonians under Alexander the Great—through the northwestern part of India and the upper reaches of the Indus River introduced fresh stimuli.

Still, it is interesting to note that according to one view India has tended to be isolated and passive in whatever exchanges took place. Geography certainly played an important role in this since the subcontinent is surrounded on east and west by seas and cut off at the top by the Himalayas, the world's loftiest mountains. New cultures have always entered India through the sole cultural crossroads the region had at its disposal, the northwestern region, India's window to the world. Though some changes were made by the opening of sea routes to India in the early centuries of the Christian Era, the total picture remained unchanged until modern times.

It is precisely because India has been at the receiving end of most cultural exchanges that the deliberate efforts of King Ashoka to carry Buddhism to the West stand out in sharp relief.

KARAN SINGH: The question that you have raised regarding the relationship between India and the western world is an important one. Two aspects must be considered. Firstly, the prevalent theory holds that the Aryan tribes moved from Central Asia in two great migrations, one westward into Iran and the other southward into India. The similarities between the Vedic texts and the *gathas* of Zarathustra are striking, though, curiously enough, they have never been adequately researched.

The second point involves the interaction between the Aryans and the existing civilization in India. The old theory that the people with whom the Aryans came into contact were barbarians is now seen to be a narrow and unsatisfactory approach. In fact the extensive remains of what is known as the Indus valley civilization clearly show that the pre-Aryan peoples in India had achieved a high standard of cultural and economic development. A third important, though not dominant, element consisting of the indigenous tribes inhabited India perhaps from even before the time of the Indus valley civilization. Indian culture as we know it today, including Hinduism, is the result of a creative mingling of these three great streams.

I have referred to this because it is important in an understanding of India's relations with the outside world, particularly the West. I do not agree with the view that 'India has tended to be isolated and passive in whatever exchanges took place'. On the contrary, India has always been at the crossroads of great trade routes and movements of civilization, and, far from being passive, has been creatively responsive to influences from outside. A Vedic line 'Aa no bhadra kratavo yantu vishwatah'—'Let noble thoughts come to us from every side'—well describes the Indian attitude. This was chosen by the late Dr K. M. Munshi, an eminent scholar and political figure, as the motto for the Bharatiya Vidya Bhavan, which he set up four decades ago as an international forum for the study and development of Indian culture.

IKEDA: In saying that India has tended to remain passive in exchanges, I was attempting to say that she has never been aggressive. Throughout her history, India has never sent military expeditions outside the subcontinent with the aim of extending her boundaries.

King Ashoka did, however, make considerable efforts to spread Buddhism beyond his own realms. From his famous rock inscriptions it is known that this great king dispatched envoys to carry the Buddhist teachings to five kingdoms including Syria, Egypt and Macedonia.

Contacts between Buddhism and the Greeks are known to have begun at an early time. Greeks in the army of Alexander the Great learned of Buddhism from the Indian people. Some professed faith in it or even became Buddhist monks. Furthermore, considerable documentary evidence from Sri Lanka and in the Pali language indicates that Buddhist missionaries were active among the Greeks during Ashoka's time. For instance, the Ceylonese history *Mahavamsa* mentions a *Yavana* (Greek) elder named Dhammaraccita, who arrived from the *Yavana* capital *Alasanda* with thirty thousand *bhikkhu* or Buddhist monks. A Pali text, the *Samatapasadika*, speaks of a *Yavana* named Maha-Dhammarakkhita, who carried a sutra to the Punjab and to Bactria, where he taught and converted many people. As a consequence of this kind of activity and of Ashoka's deliberate policy of propagating the teachings, Buddhism travelled westward to exert a subtle influence on the religions and philosophies of Greece and Rome. Various things are now being unearthed to elucidate this influence.

For instance, documentary evidence suggests that Buddhism may have reached the British Isles before Christianity. A passage in Origen's annotations on the Book of Ezekiel says that the Druids and the Buddhists in England had long ago inclined the people to accept Christianity by teaching monotheism. Such mention suggests that Buddhism had moved far west at an early date. Gandhara sculpture has been unearthed from Roman walls in Northumberland; and a small figure of Buddha has been found in Sweden.

Elsewhere and from other historical periods too, evidence of Buddhist influence is being uncovered. For example, the priests of the Jewish sect called the Therapeutae, who lived near Alexandria in Egypt in the early part of the Christian Era, reflect possibly Buddhist elements in their way of life, in which meditation and vegetarianism played prominent roles. Scholars are pointing to Buddhist-influenced characteristics in the life-style of the Essenic Jews, who lived on the shores of the Dead Sea from the second century BC till about the second century of the Christian Era. Though it is probably far-fetched to say, as some have, that Christ himself was influenced by Buddhism in the development of his own teachings, it is quite reasonable to identify Buddhist elements in the theology of the Alexandrian Christians, especially Clement and Origen. For instance, their theology includes the ideas of karmic transmigration, absence of the absolute self, and cause-and-effect relations. Moreover, it tends to be syncretic and more pantheistic than monotheistic and reveals the kind of tolerance of other faiths that is characteristic of Buddhism.

KARAN SINGH: The interactions between India and the West have been numerous, beginning in the mists of antiquity and coming down to the British advent in more recent times. Because most of the scholars working on Indian history have been Western-oriented, they have concentrated their research mainly on this aspect. The other aspect of India's relations with the East has not yet received adequate attention.

The great figure of Emperor Ashoka indeed stands as a

landmark in India's relations with the East, and you are right to remark upon his efforts to spread Buddhism far and wide. In my view, he was more successful in the East than the West because eastern peoples have always been more receptive to new ideas whereas the West has been largely influenced by the rigid, monotheistic Semitic religions, whether Zarathustrianism or Judaism, Christianity or Islam. This whole area, of course, needs much deeper study.

IKEDA: There are some puzzling points about westward Buddhist influence. First of all, it is always related to primitive—that is Theravada—teachings and never to Mahayana philosophy. This may be because, at the time of the evolution of Mahayana, the Parthian empire blocked western intercourse with India. Is it possible that climate or life-style had something to do with this failure? It is tempting to think so, since Buddhism has apparently found a greater welcome in East and Southeast Asia, where agriculture—notably rice culture—is the major source of sustenance. Why, in your opinion, did primitive, and not Mahayana, Buddhism influence the West? How can we explain Buddhism's inability to take root in the western world?

KARAN SINGH: I am not sure whether the use of the word *primitive* to describe Hinayana Buddhism is desirable, because it has a certain negative connotation in the English language. Nonetheless, as you say, the influence of Buddhism in the West seems to have been more effective in the early stages of its development before the Mahayana cult had become prominent. Interaction between Buddhism and early Christianity was deeper than is generally realized, and probably translations of Sanskrit texts into Pehlevi, Arabic, Syrian and then into western languages helped to bring such elements of Buddhist thought as the Jataka stories into western consciousness.

Before I close my remarks on this question, I would like to make an important point. While the growth of Buddhism in East Asia, initiated by Ashoka, has been reasonably well studied, it is important to remember that there was an equally powerful stream of Hindu influence to many of these countries, including Cambodia, Malaysia and Indonesia. Probably the greatest Hindu temple in the world is in Ankor Wat, Cambodia; and, to this day, Hinduism flourishes on the Indonesian island of Bali. I find it curious that while the great Borobudur in Jogjakarta is known throughout the world, the even more impressive Hindu temple at Parambaran, in the same town, is hardly known outside of Indonesia. To understand the Indian influence upon Southeast Asia, one must take into account not only the Buddhist but also the Hindu tradition.

7. The Pacifism of King Ashoka

IKEDA: The late Count Richard E. Coudenhove-Kalergi—a true Pan-European who is sometimes called the father of the European Economic Community—once remarked that, of all the great kings of history, Ashoka is most deserving of respect. (In Count Coudenhove-Kalergi's later years, he and I met on two occasions and published a collection of dialogues entitled *Civilization—East and West*.) As a Buddhist, I too was attracted to the flowering culture of the Mauryan dynasty from an early age and felt especially interested in the figure of this great king. The first unifier of India, Ashoka abandoned warfare and adopted a policy of pacific rule not very long after his ascension to the throne.

Many colourful stories are told about him. It is said in Buddhist texts that, because in a former life he made an offering of a cake made of sand to the Buddha, he acquired such merit that he was destined to be born a Great Wheel-rolling King (*Chakravarti-raja*) who rules by righteousness alone. There are stories to the effect that Ashoka was a terrible tyrant in his young years. Later, however, he became a devout Buddhist and earned the title *Dharmashoka*, or Ashoka of the Law. His famous rock and pillar inscriptions tell us that he erected 84,000 Buddhist stupas throughout the land, sponsored the compilation of the Buddhist texts, and himself made many pilgrimages.

These inscriptions, of which more than forty have already been definitely identified, contain a programme for peace that, more than twenty-two centuries later, is still extraordinary.

The rock inscriptions tell us that, stricken by remorse at seeing ten thousand people killed and fifteen thousand taken prisoner when he attacked Kalinga (modern Orissa), King Ashoka resolved to rule through the Buddhist Law. This took place eight years after he had ascended the throne. It is likely that, he had already encountered the teachings of Buddhism. Ten years after his enthronement, he made a pilgrimage to the place where Gautama Buddha attained enlightenment. Consistent with his change of heart, Ashoka did more than make pilgrimages. He reduced his armed forces to ceremonial guards and, realizing that without arms he would be unable to defend himself from foreign attack, sent envoys of peace to surrounding nations throughout a wide area. Furthermore, he made his appeals to neighboring peoples in their own languages. An Ashoka pillar, which astounded historians and archaeologists when first discovered, bears the king's pacific message in Greek and Aramaic for the sake of the many Greeks and Iranians who then lived in the region from northwest India to the deserts further west.

King Ashoka's peace drive was international, in keeping with Buddhist teachings, which transcend race or nation. What is your opinion of Ashoka's attitude and achievements in connection with the establishment of peace?

KARAN SINGH: The Emperor Ashoka is one of the outstanding figures not only of Indian, but of world history. He is rightly looked upon as the first royal patron of Buddhism, and it was largely through his efforts that Buddhism came to occupy the prominent position that it did in India and abroad. It is often forgotten that he was the grandson of Chandragupta

Maurya, the first great Hindu emperor in Indian history, who founded his capital in Pataliputra, now Patna.

The life of Ashoka, especially his dramatic conversion to pacifism after the slaughter at Kalinga, is well known throughout the world, as is his unique contribution to spreading the message of peace. It is quite remarkable that he erected so many Buddhist stupas, sponsored the compilation of Buddhist texts, sent missionaries, including his son Mahendra and daughter Sanghamitra, throughout the world, and spent the second half of his life in propagating the Buddha's message. Indeed, in the vast and varied galaxy of rulers in India, he perhaps ranks next only to Sri Rama himself, who is considered by Hindus to have been an incarnation of Vishnu and whose establishment of Rama Rajya preceded Ashoka's Dharma Rajya by many centuries.

IKEDA: There can be no doubt that reading about Ashoka's life and learning from it how this ancient king ruled in peace on the basis of Buddhist ideals can be of immense value today, when peace is of such importance.

The horror of war turned Ashoka to peace. The disastrous air raids on Tokyo and other principal cities in the late phase of World War II and the atomic bombings of Hiroshima and Nagasaki, where tens of thousands of people lost their lives, led the Japanese people to adopt a constitution renouncing belligerence and proclaiming peace. Upon regaining his freedom after having been unjustly imprisoned by the militarists, the second president of Soka Gakkai, Josei Toda, viewed the blackened ruins that had once been the city of Tokyo. This inspired him to undertake a movement for peace and the relief of human suffering based on the propagation of the teachings of the Buddhism of Nichiren Daishonin. In the more than thirty years that have passed since then, we of Soka Gakkai, now an organization of roughly ten million members, have consistently emphasized the vital importance of peace.

As a Buddhist, I travel about the world attempting to

contribute to the building of a lasting peace through work in the cultural and educational fields. Though all peoples differ in various respects, when it comes to propagating the ideal of a peaceful society on earth, we are all one.

KARAN SINGH: Your comments regarding the enhanced significance of Ashoka's message of peace in this nuclear age are extremely relevant. A single nuclear warhead now packs more explosive power than all the explosives used by both sides during the whole of World War II. A single one of these warheads is a thousand times as powerful as the bombs that cruelly obliterated Hiroshima and Nagasaki over forty years ago, and there are today at least fifty thousand such nuclear warheads in the arsenals of the world, ninety-five per cent of them belonging to the two super-powers. Our first and greatest Dharma today, therefore, is to prevent a nuclear holocaust, which would obliterate not only the human race, but also perhaps all forms of life on this planet.

During my travels throughout the world, I have been increasingly struck by the fact that western civilization, with all its great and glittering achievements, stands today on the threshold of a grave crisis. Science and technology have given man tremendous power, which, if utilized with wisdom and compassion, can abolish poverty and malnutrition, illiteracy and hunger from the face of the earth by the end of this century. The same science and technology, however, today threaten the existence of mankind, particularly when the predominent ideology is Mutually Assured Destruction (MAD).

In this context, I feel that the East can once again come to the rescue of mankind by reiterating the great ideals of the all-pervasiveness of the divine, mankind as a family, the divinity inherent in each individual and the welfare of all sections of society, which are found in the teachings of the Upanishads and of the Buddha. We must propagate these throughout the world as urgently and effectively as we possibly can.

8. *The Questions of King Milinda*

IKEDA: From about the second half of the second century BC, western civilization was introduced into India in a very dramatic way, as a whole series of Greek kings—their number is said to exceed forty—invaded northwest India. One of these kings, Menander, who at first ruled the area extending from Kabul in modern Afghanistan to Takshashila (known in classical western literature as Taxila), invaded northwest India at about this time to become beloved among the people as the philosopher-monarch Milinda. Though he used force to conquer in the early phase of his reign, the description in the famous dialogue *The Questions of King Milinda* reveals him as a true Greek ruler in the best tradition and a man open to free exchange of opinions:

'. . .Milinda by name, learned, eloquent, wise, and able; and a faithful observer, and that at the right time, of all the various acts of devotion and ceremony enjoined by his own sacred hymns concerning things past, present, and to come. Many were the arts and sciences he knew—holy tradition and secular law, the *Sankya*, Yoga, *Nyaya*, and the *Vaisheshika* systems of philosophy, arithmetic; music; medicine; the four Vedas; the *Puranas*, and the *Itihasas*; astronomy, magic, causation and spells; the art of war; poetry; conveyancing—in a word, the whole nineteen.' (*The Questions of King Milinda*, translated from Pali by T.W. Rhys Davids, Motilal Banarasidass, Delhi.)

From this passage it is possible to see that, being versed in the arts and sciences of the Grecian world, Milinda was eager to learn about the culture and philosophy of India. Some scholars today believe that he merged with the local people and learned to speak their language. Records in Pali show that he made active attempts to engage in dialogues with Brahmans, ascetics, and members of the Buddhist Order. Perhaps in doing this he was influenced by the example of Alexander the Great, who was impressed by naked Indian ascetics with whom he spoke when he was in Takshashila in

326 BC. Still it seems to have been traditional among Greek rulers to try to learn from the sages of other lands.

Apparently Milinda engaged in philosophical discussions with many learned Indians without finding anyone who could satisfy his mind until he came into contact with Nagasena, a monk-philosopher of the then flourishing Mahayana school of Buddhism. The introduction to the *The Questions of King Milinda* describes how the Order was searching for someone to take part in a dialogue with the king and suggests that Nagasena was considered most suitable. The discussions took place at Milinda's capital, a city called Sagala, which modern Japanese scholars identify as Sialkot, not far from the India-Pakistan border (and directly south of your own state of Jammu and Kashmir).

In the same book the monk Nagasena is described in the following way: '. . . leader of a company of the Order; the head of a body of disciples; the teacher of a school; famous and renowned, and highly esteemed by the people. And he was learned, clever, wise, sagacious, and able; a skilful expounder of subdued manner, but full of courage; well versed in tradition; master of the three Baskets (*Pitaka*), and erudite in Vedic lore. He was in possession of the highest (Buddhist) insight, a master of all that had been handed down in the schools, and of the various discriminations by which the most abstruse points can be explained. He knew by heart the ninefold divisions of the doctrine of the Buddha to perfection, and was equally skilled in discerning both the spirit and the letter of the World.' (Ibid.)

As Milinda was a representative example of a Grecian king well-versed in the western culture of his time, so Nagasena represented the best of the Indian philosopher-sages of that time. In its present form, *The Questions of King Milinda*, the record of the discussions between these two leaders of eastern and western culture, consists of 262 questions, though material not recorded could raise the total to 300. It took place two thousand years ago, but the dialogue preserves its natural freshness and dignity today.

Records say that, as a consequence of this dialogue, King Milinda abandoned pride and arrogance and came to entertain pure faith in the Buddhist Three Treasures (the Law, the Buddha, and the Order). Thereafter he became a lay believer and donated to the order a monastery named Milinda. It is further held that he later resigned the rule of the nation to a prince, became a monk, and disciplined himself until he became an arhat. Of course these stories have been advanced by Buddhists, but it is important to note that a Buddhist reliquary bearing the name of King Milinda has been found in the Swat region.

Do you agree with me that the story of the king's conversion to zeal for Buddhism because of the dialogue with the monk-philosopher Nagasena is not improbable? What are the extent and significance of the exchanges between East and West that took place in India at about the time of these two men?

KARAN SINGH: Without going into a long historical survey, it seems to me that western historians tend to overestimate the impact of the Greek upon Indian culture and history. That this impact was important in many ways is not denied, but in the vast sweep of Indian history—both geographical and chronological—it must be looked upon as of marginal importance. In fact, Menander ruled only in parts of northern India, and the vast bulk of the subcontinent, stretching all the way down to the Indian Ocean, was hardly affected by this. Perhaps that explains why he is seldom mentioned in Pali works other than the *Milindapanha*.

Having said this, I will add that King Milinda was obviously a man of remarkable capacity, representing the rare combination of prowess in the field of battle and erudite philosophical capacity. His famous dialogue with the Buddhist sage Nagasena reminds us of the earlier Upanishadic dialogues between King Janaka and the great sage Yajnyavalkya. In turn, Nagasena was obviously a man not only of deep learning, but also of immense wisdom. You are right to say that the meeting between Milinda and Nagasena represents the East-West dialogue at its noblest.

The story of King Milinda's conversion to Buddhism as a result of this dialogue is certainly not improbable. There are many instances in which men who are actively involved in politics and warfare undergo a sudden, alchemical, transformation when exposed to persons of wisdom and spiritual attainment.

The Indo-Greek mutual impact represents a significant event in the long history of East-West dialogue. Several scholars have studied this from the western viewpoint and perhaps tend to exaggerate its importance. Some Indian scholars tend to play down its significance. A historian like Arnold Toynbee seems to have taken a balanced and fair view. I suggest that this is a fertile field for further study, specially from the eastern (Hindu/Buddhist) standpoint.

9. Gandhara Culture

IKEDA: The Gandhara Culture, which flourished in the vicinity of Peshawar (in modern Pakistan), from the first to the fourth or fifth century of the Christian Era, is especially noteworthy for two reasons. First, it represents a conflux of the oriental culture of India and the occidental culture of Greece in its Hellenistic form. Second, this conflux was effected by the Kushan people, whose background is largely mysterious. These people, who occupied more territory than any other Indian dynasty, are referred to as *Guishuang* or Greater *Yuezhi* in Chinese records and are thought to have lived, until the third century BC, as nomads in the vast region between Dunhuang and the Qilianshan Mountains. In the first half of the second century BC, pursued by the people called *Xiongnu*, they fled westward to pass along the Silk Road and settle in what is now Afghanistan.

During the reign of King Ashoka, in the third century BC, Buddhism had already been introduced to the Gandhara region; and it is likely that by the time of the arrival of the

Kushans, many of the Greeks, Iranians, Shakas and Parthians living there had become Buddhists and had created a new, distinctive culture. In other words, Gandhara had become a centre of civilizational crossroads and a melting pot for many races, including indigenous Indo-Aryans, descendants of Alexander the Great, and various nomadic peoples.

In the second century, with the establishment of a second Kushan empire by the great king Kanishka, Buddhist culture in Gandhara reached its apex. The empire itself attained maximum territorial limits: from what was Magadha in the east to Afghanistan in the west, from the Deccan Heights in the south to modern Soviet Central Asia in the north, and to the oases on the southern edges of the Chinese Tarim Basin. Gandhara Buddhist culture not only extended throughout this immense terrain, but also exerted influence on many surrounding peoples.

Buddhist tradition claims that, before coming to Gandhara, Kanishka had been a member of the group of people called Lesser *Yuezhi* and had lived in Khotan. The renowned Chinese monk and pilgrim Xuanzang (AD 600–64) claims that Kanishka sponsored the forth Council for compiling and collating the Buddhist texts at Kashmir, to which you have referred. Possibly Kanishka came to Gandhara by way of the southern edge of the Kunlun Mountains and Kashmir, whose attractions he must have known, and which he chose as the council site when it became clear that extremes of temperature made Gandhara unsuitable.

In the first year after his accession to the throne, Kanishka built a large stupa to house relics of the Buddha in Purshapala (modern Peshawar) the spring and summer capital of his kingdom. Both Faxian and Xuangzang, two of China's most illustrious pilgrim monks, remark on having seen this stupa.

In moments of relaxation from cares of state, Kanishka was fond of studying Buddhism with monks and scholars whom he invited regularly to his palace. One of them was probably the brilliant Buddhist poet and author of the five-volume *Deeds of the Buddha*, Ashvaghosha, whom

Kanishka brought back with him after an attack on the kingdom of Magadha, in east India, not long after he became king.

To the Kushan kingdom and the Gandhara culture belongs the credit for producing numerous Buddha and Bodhisattva statues, an immense number of which have been excavated at Maurya in India, at Taxila and Peshawar in Pakistan, and at Hadda in Afghanistan. As you know, in the earliest period, Buddhists did not make statues representing the Buddha.

KARAN SINGH: Gandhara culture, which in fact traces its name to the city of Kandhahar in Northern India (now Pakistan), is indeed one of the highlights of Indian civilization and represents a harmonious mingling of Greek and Indian traditions. From the point of view of sculpture, Gandhara art played a crucial role. Neither among the Aryans nor the early Buddhists was there a tradition of representing the deity in human form, though this was prevalent in the ancient Indus valley civilization. The superb sculptural influence of the Greeks, represented in the Gandhara School, reintroduced human figures into the Indian religious tradition—both Buddhist and Hindu. As is well known, for many centuries Indian Buddhists refrained from depicting the Buddha in human form and represented him only by such symbols as the Bodhi tree, the Wheel of the Law (Dharma Chakra), his footprints, his umbrella, or an empty throne. With the Gandhara school which flourished under the patronage of the Kushan kings, however, the great traditions of figurative sculpture were revived in a most dramatic and impressive manner.

The most famous and impressive ruler of the Kushan empire—and undoubtedly one of the great figures in Indian history—was the emperor Kanishka. In the first volume of his monumental *Story of Civilization*, Will Durant describes Kanishka as 'almost the second Ashoka'. In his reign many religions flourished, but his special reverence was reserved for Buddhism and was expressed not only in the efflorescence of Buddhist art, but also in the Fourth International Buddhist Council held in Kashmir.

IKEDA: Scholars in both the East and the West are still trying—so far without success—to explain the origin of statues of Buddha. One apparently valid theory claims that statues were permitted because of the need of offering something concrete to help Greeks, from the West, understand Buddhist teachings.

I should very much like to hear your opinions on the historical significance of the Gandhara civilization.

KARAN SINGH: Whereas the Greeks were expert in beautiful depictions of the human form, of which the Sun God Apollo was considered to be the epitome, their sculpture tended to lack the dimension projecting not just the outer beauty of the deity, but also its inner luminosity. The creative fusion making this possible—and well represented by the remarkable Mathura and Sarnath Buddhas (5th century AD)—took place as a result of what may be called Indianization of the Greek tradition.

The question regarding explanation of Buddhist statues seems to me to have a fairly clear answer. There are many ways in which the individual can make contact with the Divine. In reply to earlier questions, I have pointed out the four major paths (or Yogas) which Hinduism offers for this union between the human and the Divine. One of these is the *Bhakti Marg*, the way of devotion; and the history of the human race shows clearly that devotion can best be invoked and expressed when the Divine is represented in anthropomorphic form. Some remarkable men like Plato or Shankara can indeed develop awareness of the divine through contemplation of ideas alone, but for the vast bulk of humanity a human figure seems to be the most acceptable object of worship.

It is interesting that both Hinduism and Buddhism started without human representation but in due course developed an extremely rich and varied pantheon. The development of representational statues of the Buddha should, therefore, be looked upon as a logical sequence hastened by Greek impact. A significant study needs to be made of the psychological differences between religions encouraging the use of human figures in worship—Hinduism, Buddhism, Jainism and Roman Catholicism—and those stern Semitic religions that forbid it—Judaism, Islam and some forms of Christianity. Perhaps the use of the human figure, especially when male and female figures are employed in combination, as in Hinduism, has the effect of humanizing the worshipper.

CHAPTER FOUR

The Fate of Buddhism in India and Elsewhere

1. Causes of Decline

IKEDA: For more than a thousand years, from the reign of King Ashoka, in the third century BC, until about the eighth or ninth century of the Christian Era, Buddhism flourished in India and brought to flower a splendid culture, illustrated in an amazing way by the number, scale and artistic value of the Buddhist ruins, including those of the famous Nalanda University and those dating from the time of King Kanishka, to be seen today in India, Pakistan and Afghanistan. Especially worthy of notice are the virtual treasure troves of temples and stupas at Gandhara in the Peshawar region of Afghanistan, the ruins of Taxila near Rawalpindi, and those in the valley of Swat in the Peshawar district.

Such monuments as the great stone Buddha at Bamiyan, Afghanistan (which, fifty-three metres high, is the largest figure of its kind in the world), the Hadda ruins near the Pakistan border, and groups of other ruins near the border of the Soviet Union clearly indicate how great must have been the religious faith of the Buddhists who built them.

At present, however, there are no Buddhists in these regions, all of which were invaded and converted by Muslims. From the absence of Buddhists in these zones and their persistence in such places as Burma and the Indo-China peninsula, which were not invaded by Muslims, it seems undeniable that destruction at the hands of the faithful of Islam was an important cause of the downfall of Buddhism in this part of the world.

Hinduism, however, was preserved in India in spite of the Islamic invasion. Why was this? What are your thoughts about the complex of elements that brought about the demise of Buddhism in India?

KARAN SINGH: The decline of Buddhism in India was the outcome of a long, complex and multidimensional process. Briefly, we can identify four major elements which contributed to this decline.

The first set of causes can be traced to internal factors. After his passing, the great spiritual and moral impetus of the Buddha gradually faded away; and Buddhism fell prey to sectarian disputes, which often became as bitter as those between Buddhists and non-Buddhists. This naturally led to an erosion in Buddhism's appeal. Simultaneously, with a sharp decline in royal patronage, Buddhism lost its main economic support. The fact that the monasteries were largely clustered around urban centres and did not have deep roots in the countryside endorses the view that the faith had become unduly dependent upon political patronage.

Secondly, the Buddha was always reluctant to admit women into the monastic order; and it was only at the repeated intervention of his closest disciple Ananda that he agreed to do so. While this was in some ways a truly revolutionary step, it carried within it the seeds of grave trouble in the future. As long as the tremendous spiritual power of the Buddha remained prevalent, the system worked well. Through the centuries, however, growing laxity of monastic rules and degeneration in the moral and spiritual attainments of the monks and nuns inevitably occurred. From literary evidence it would appear that this had become very glaring by the seventh and eighth centuries of the Christian Era. Several literary works composed at that time hold the monasteries up to ridicule. This surely tended to erode the prestige and influence of the monastic order among the general public and thus hastened its ultimate collapse.

IKEDA: Both these causes arose from within the Order. Indeed, during his lifetime, Gautama Buddha warned his disciples to be on guard against the enemy within and said metaphorically that the lion can be killed by a worm dwelling inside its own body.

Perhaps Buddhism found it difficult to survive because it demands stern discipline in lofty ideas supported by a high degree of spiritual tension. Human beings find the road to degeneration easy but the upward path to improvement difficult.

KARAN SINGH: Now to my third element. As I have pointed out earlier in this dialogue, although it set itself up as a new and independent religion, Buddhism retained close links with Hinduism, from which it originally emerged. Hinduism has a remarkable capacity to absorb other faiths, rather like an ocean that absorbs the mightiest of rivers without overflowing. The factors mentioned earlier coincided with a powerful resurgence of Hinduism led by the great philosopher-reformer Adi Shankaracharya (eighth century of the Christian Era). This must have played a major role in the decline of Buddhism in India, particularly as some of its prominent tenets like abolition of animal sacrifice were adopted by Hinduism itself.

Finally, as you have stated, the terrible Islamic invasion which began in the eighth century and ravaged India for many centuries thereafter, delivered the final *coup de grâce* to Buddhism in India. The ruthless destruction of Vikramshila, and the massacre of its nuns and monks by Muslims in 1203 symbolizes this aspect. It is important to remember, however, that Hinduism too was subjected to equally ruthless destruction by the Muslims but survived both because of its deep roots among the people, specially in the rural areas, and because of its profound philosophical resilience. The manner in which Hinduism not only survived the Muslim impact but continued to develop new dimensions through the centuries contrasts sharply with the inability of Buddhism to withstand the Islamic wave in India.

2. The Perils of Urban Religions

IKEDA: The Soviet archaeologist M. E. Masson has said that, whereas the influence of Buddhism is immediately apparent in major Bactrian urban centres, no trace of the Indian religion at all can be found in such rural towns as Kej-Kobad Shakh. Though it pertains not directly to India, but to a neighbouring region, this statement indicates the urban nature of Buddhism. The nature of the Order after the death of Gautama Buddha too is an important reason why Buddhism developed as an urban religion.

The Buddha skilfully explained his enlightenment to others. His outstanding personality lent persuasive power to his words, which were richly amplified by means of metaphors and replete with compassion. These qualities enabled him to explain difficult teachings to even the uneducated. The sutras tell us that not all his disciples were learned men like Shariputra and Maudgalyayana but that some were people of little or no education at all. After his death, however, the teachings evolved into an elaborate, difficult body of doctrines, the complex differences among which inevitably led to the splitting of the Order into many rival factions whose conflicts took them farther and farther away from Gautama Buddha's truth.

The Buddha taught in Prakrit, a vernacular language that the masses understood. He disliked fruitless ideological debating and, although he adjusted his reactions to the abilities of his audience, when his disciples asked questions that had no relation to liberation from actual human sorrow, remained silent. The story of the poisoned arrow illustrates his attitude in such matters.

Once Gautama Buddha was asked about the survival of the individual self after death. He is said to have replied in this way. Suppose a man has been shot with a poisoned arrow. Refusing to extract the weapon until investigations ascertain the identity of the man who shot it, whether he is tall or short, and the material from which the arrow is made, gives the poison time to do its work; and the wounded man dies. The important thing is to pull the arrow out and treat the injured man. Similarly, it is important, not to discuss the continued existence of the individual self after death, but to liberate living creatures from the poison of delusion now.

Gautama Buddha's primary concern was for the practical elimination of suffering. He spoke in easy words that all people could understand, and his message spread far and wide.

KARAN SINGH: Any religion which bases itself upon the teachings of a single person, no matter how noble and elevated, runs the risk of declining when the original radiance of the teacher gradually grows pale through the efflux of time. The Buddha was one of mankind's most remarkable teachers, and it is astounding how great a transformation he was able to bring about within his own lifetime. His teachings, replete with wisdom and compassion, are among the great treasures of human consciousness.

The Buddha's famous parable about the arrow is certainly well taken, but there seems to me to be no harm if, while pulling out the arrow and treating the injured man, there is a parallel attempt to find out who the aggressor was so that he can be prevented from launching a second attack.

IKEDA: As long as the therapy precedes the investigation. Furthermore, it might be said that searching for the criminal is the work of the police and not that of the doctor. At any rate, as I have already said, Gautama Buddha would have adjusted his approach and comments to the nature of his audience.

Just prior to his death, Gautama Buddha had instructed his followers to rely solely on the Law. The Order's subsequent striving to grasp the accurate meaning of the teachings is therefore understandable; nonetheless, the desire for accuracy led to extensive scholarly interpretations, which in turn generated a body of difficult doctrines responsible for isolating the teachings from the ordinary people. And this was an error. Separation from the ordinary people was further widened when, at the fourth council, held under the patronage of King Kanishka, the teachings were codified in Sanskrit, the classical Indian language found in holy Brahman writings and the Vedas. When this happened, Buddhism became the property of a limited group.

In my opinion, though sophisticated philosophical systems are sometimes needed to deal with their ramifications, essentially all truths are to be found in simple, clear, practical principles. When a philosophy loses sight of simple fundamentals, it loses its life-force. Do you agree that, when it committed this error, the Buddhist Order isolated itself from the ordinary people and opened the way to decline and finally failure in India? It seems to me that Buddhism became a scholarly system compelled to survive only in urban institutions of learning.

KARAN SINGH: The very length and diversity of the Buddha's teachings lent themselves, after his passing away, to a variety of interpretations. Various sects developed and stressed different elements of the teachings; and in due course the original radiance was lost in the morass of scholarly disputes and interpretations.

It is quite true that a purely scholarly religion is unable to fulfil the inner needs of the common man. This does not mean, however, that complex philosophical questions should remain unacknowledged or unanswered or that the approach should become simplistic instead of simple.

The Buddha was silent when asked about the fate of the individual soul after death. Hinduism clearly postulates the survival of the Atman after the death of the physical body. A famous verse (II-22) in the Bhagavadgita says: 'Just as a man casts off worn-out clothes and puts on new ones, so does the embodied self cast off its worn-out body and enter others which are new.' To my mind this clear and unequivocal statement is a more satisfying position to take.

IKEDA: It is not that Buddhism has nothing to say about life after death, but it warns against making abstract deliberation on the subject an issue of major importance. Depending on whether the party being addressed is of a philosophical bent, enjoys playing with abstract ideas, or is of a practical turn of mind, Buddhism has various different teachings to offer on the subject.

KARAN SINGH: All religions, and especially Hinduism, function on several different levels. There is the philosophical level, the organizational or monastic level, and what may be called the popular level. In Buddhism the great prayer *Buddham Sharanam Gachhami; Sangham Sharanam Gachhami; Dhamman Sharanam Gachhami* represents these three great levels.

IKEDA: Interestingly, although it has been strong on the philosophical and organizational levels, Buddhism has tended to be weak on the popular level. Hinduism, on the other hand, while weak on the organizational level, has been strong on the popular level.

3. Isolation from the People

IKEDA: Gautama Buddha instructed his disciples to have pity on the world and to travel about working for the advantage and happiness of all human beings. During his lifetime, the Buddha himself travelled and preached among the people.

The origin of Buddhist monasteries is said to lie in the custom of halting in travel for the rainy season. Originally, this break was dictated by the desire to avoid trampling on new buds and shoots emerging at this time. In the first part of his mission, the Buddha refused to take the rainy-season break. He later conceded to custom owing to criticism from the devotees of other religions and to avoid being misunderstood. The Buddha's disciples banded together to form the Order, or Sangha. As time went on, however, the number of lay, as well as monk, believers increased. When this happened, lay followers began making contributions to the

Order; and it became customary for new monks to settle down in monasteries, where they trained and disciplined themselves. Two main reasons account for the shift from the former unsettled, mendicant way of life of Buddhist monks to that of permanent residence in religious establishments. The first was the need for a place in which to engage in scholarly examination of the teachings. The second was the desire to remain near cities where lived the lay believers who had become the Order's financial mainstay.

Monastic life physically isolated the Order from the ordinary people. And this was a departure from the Buddha's original intent. He had instructed members of the Order to go out among the people and, with profound self-awareness and enlightenment, to travel separate ways—no two monks taking the same road.

KARAN SINGH: The Buddha being one of the great teachers of mankind and having founded a faith based upon certain specific doctrines, it was only to be expected that he should pay special attention to the education and training of his followers. The development of the monasteries largely revolved around the necessity to train neophytes. This system was known as *Nissaya*, a period of learning which preceded the attainment of the full status of a monk. It has an interesting parallel to the Hindu concept of brahmacharya, during which the disciples live with their Guru for twelve years from the age of six or seven. A valuable comparative study should be made of the Hindu and Buddhist traditions in this regard.

IKEDA: No doubt, a novice monk requires a period of development and training before he is able to teach others effectively. But the Buddha's plan was to combine education with actual practice, not to provide special, isolated training settlements.

Gautama Buddha's teaching was one of enlightenment to the brilliant life within each individual and the establishment of true happiness on the basis of that enlightenment. In other words, essentially, Gautama Buddha's teachings abide in the mind of each individual and not in some organization with special authority. In India, however, Buddhism fell into a kind of authoritarianism. It lost the brilliant force of life it had possessed in Gautama Buddha's time and thus separated itself from the hearts of the people. This point, too, played a part in the downfall, which was precipitated by the destruction of temples and the killing of monks and nuns at the hands of the Muslims.

KARAN SINGH: Once Buddhism began attracting large numbers of lay and monastic disciples, it was inevitable that institutionalization should take place. We must remember that, during the Buddha's own lifetime, the number of his actual disciples must always have been quite small, although vast numbers of people gathered to listen to his discourses. With the tremendous expansion that took place after his death, the only option was for the Sangha to organize itself around monasteries, which often developed into great seats of learning. Elaborate texts dealing with various aspects of monastic life developed. The well-known Sanskrit work Saptadashabhumi Shastra (400 of the Christian Era) is only one of them. The logical culmination of these monastic centres was the setting up of the great monastic universities at Nalanda, Valabhi, and Vikramshila. These were among the greatest educational institutions ever established in human history, and their destruction by Muslim invaders must rank as one of the greatest tragedies of mankind.

IKEDA: Such great centres of learning as Nalanda and Vikramshila came into being as a natural consequence of the profundity of the content of Buddhist teachings. They do, as you say, represent pinnacles in human civilization, and I am by no means averse to praising them. I do think, however, that too much stress was placed on their importance at the expense of other considerations.

A philosophy, no matter how profound, if not put into actual practice degenerates into vapid ideology. Thoughts that find no expression in actions end up in a world of self-contained complacency.

In my opinion, Buddhism should be practised in such a way as to enable human beings to live vigorous and full lives. Doctrines must be put to practical use if they are to have maximum meaning. (The organization of which I am a member combines teaching and practical action in various ways, one of which is a discussion meeting where we study the doctrines of Buddhism and share with one another our own experiences or the way those doctrines can be put into effect in daily life.)

KARAN SINGH: Though perhaps Buddhism itself is not a branch of learning, scholarship must remain one of its important elements. If I may revert to my earlier description of the four Yogas in Hinduism, I feel that any great religion needs scholarship, devotion, spiritual practice, and vigorous external activity in equal measure. Neglecting any of these four elements throws the system into an imbalance. The relationship between doctrine and practice should essentially be a symbiotic one. Doctrine without practice becomes sterile, and practice without doctrine becomes chaotic and meaningless.

4. Wealth and Decay

IKEDA: You have said that theoretical chaos within the Order cost Buddhism the respect of the ordinary people and that this is one of the causes of the religion's downfall in India. Although agreeing that this element must be taken into consideration, I see the issue of wealth as a cause of degradation in wider measure.

Believing that the cause of human unhappiness lay in attachment to property, Gautama Buddha forbade the accumulation of wealth and, abiding by his own precept, begged his food for the remainder of his days. After his death, however, his disciples gradually drifted away from his teachings of charity to others and of religious practices designed to prevent them from being controlled by such passions as greed. With the establishment of monasteries, contributions that formerly had gone to individual mendicant monks began going to these organizations, which soon amassed huge fortunes. Tenant incomes from spacious lands donated to monasteries became the monks' livelihoods. In *A History of India*, Romila Thapar comments, '... . now they ate regular meals in vast monastic refectories. Monasteries were built either adjoining a town or else on some beautiful and secluded hillside far removed from the clamour of cities. Secluded monasteries were sufficiently well endowed to enable the monks to live comfortably. The Buddhist Order thus tended to move away from the common people and isolate itself, which in turn diminished much of its religious strength, a development which one suspects the Buddha would not have found acceptable.' Vast sums contributed to monastic organizations seem to have been frequently lent out at interest. Ultimately, monastic wealth became so great that it was necessary to hire specialists to manage it. As might be expected, in time people came to join the Order for the seclusion and security of the life its monasteries offered. Misfits ostracized from society for one reason or another fled to the monastic way of life. In Gautama Buddha's time, he and all the other monks had begged and had been missionaries striving for the good of the people at large. With the establishment of religious authoritarianism, however, monks lost contact with the people and underwent religious discipline solely for their own sake. The French specialist in Indian studies Sylvain Levi says in his book *Humanism Boudique* that, if the Muslims wanted to put an end to the life of Buddhism, it was sufficient for them to burn and destroy the Buddhist temples. Like Buddhism, Brahmanism too had its Order and temples, its places of concealment for meditation and research. It, too, was supported on the basis of an established set of strict precepts. But the loss of temples did not deprive the Brahmans of either their ceremonies and rituals or their followers. The case with Buddhism, as

Sylvain Levi points out, was quite different. The temple was
the centre, the heart and soul of Buddhism. Without temples,
there would be no priests, and without priests there would be
no way to teach believers.

Though the times and the society are different, what Levi
says about Buddhism in India in that epoch is significant for
us today.

KARAN SINGH: Although sometimes wealth does lead to
degradation, I feel that a blanket condemnation of the
monasteries is not really fair. The developments you have
pointed out resulting in the growth in the wealth and
influence of monasteries can be seen in other religions too,
specially in Roman Catholicism. But I have not seen it
argued that the Church of Rome was responsible for the decay
of Christianity. Certainly when such institutions become
centres of exploitation rather than service, when wealth
becomes an end in itself rather than a means to further the
welfare of humanity, when internecine intrigue and infight-
ing consume the energy that should be flowing outward
towards humanity in service and compassion, the whole
system falls into disrepute. The history of the Roman
Catholic Church itself in the Middle Ages, when the papacy
went through a series of schisms and scandals, illustrates this
point.

It is significant that while both Gautama Buddha and Jesus
Christ were strongly against the accumulation of material
wealth, organizations founded around their teachings rapidly
became among the wealthiest in the world. The situation in
Hinduism was somewhat different because of its pluralistic
nature. Here too great temples were constructed, and whole
cities—such as Srirangam and Madurai in South India—
revolve around the great temples. Many of these were richly
endowed by the rulers with land and jewels; and indeed, after
the Muslim advent, these endowments became counter-
productive in that they attracted a special combination of
fanaticism and greed resulting in constant destruction. The

great Hindu temple at Somnath in western India, for example, was attacked on eighteen occasions, and was reconstructed only after we gained independence from the British. Nonetheless, Hinduism was able to withstand these assaults because, in the ultimate analysis, the source of its vitality lay in the internal spirit rather than external organization.

Another point to be made is that, since both Buddhism and Christianity are proselytizing religions, wealthy organizational backing is more important to them than to Hinduism. Religion must grow in intimate relations with the ordinary people and must be constantly refined and reintegrated through actual practice. A certain degree of institutionalization is, however, essential for academic and missionary work. Fortunately Hinduism's lack of an organized church allows more creativity and flexibility to evolve in the light of changing circumstances. It also makes the entire system less vulnerable to attack and destruction, because its centres of inspiration are widely dispersed and cannot be wiped out in a single blow.

IKEDA: As evidence of both accumulated wealth and the weakening of the bonds between Indian Buddhists and the ordinary people, Professor Hajime Nakamura of Tokyo University examined artifacts excavated from stupas dating from the time of the Mauryan dynasty and has shown that the contributors of offerings to these Buddhist towers came largely from the capitalist class of large landowners and merchants and from the mercantile and artisan levels of society. No farmer peasants are listed among them at all.

Professor Hiroshi Iwamoto, of Kyoto University, has categorized the names of 165 monks listed in three sutras according to social class and has shown that, of the names given, ninety-three were Brahmans, forty were Kshatriyas, twenty-eight were Vaishyas, and none were Shudras. In other words, in this group of monks, eighty per cent came from the ruling classes.

It was precisely because Buddhists came largely from the

ruling urban intelligentsia that the Muslim invasions practically annihilated them. The invaders were intent on capturing the cities and subjugating the rural population. But relations between them and the farming peasants were strictly economic and did not penetrate to personal matters like religion. In the cities, where authority was inevitably centered, however, everything had to be swept clean and re-established according to the invaders' policies. Buddhism was one of the elements of urban society that had to be destroyed. The fate of Buddhism in India illustrates the truth that, though a philosophy or religion requires a spirit of renovation and renewal, to persist and endure it must be deeply rooted in the hearts of the ordinary masses of humanity.

KARAN SINGH: As I mentioned earlier, Buddhism was a largely urban phenomenon and was thus highly vulnerable to foreign conquest. The caste composition of the monks worked out by Professor Iwamoto is most revealing. Although Buddhism began as a movement against Brahman domination, these figures show that almost sixty per cent of the monks at that time were in fact Brahmans, which clearly illustrates that Buddhism had become largely dependent upon the urban intelligentsia. Further, unlike Hinduism, in which religious teachers dwelt among the masses, the Buddhist tradition was to segregate monks in monasteries. Although they were enjoined to serve the people, it would appear that, in due course, they developed into a sort of burden upon society. It is one thing to serve food to the occasional mendicant; it is quite another to have to sustain, on a permanent basis, many thousands of monks not directly involved in productive work.

For any philosophy or religion to survive and retain its dynamism, it is essential that a constant renovation and renewal take place and, as you say, the roots in the hearts of the masses must be deep. This can be the case only when a steady stream of men and women of spiritual enlightenment, wisdom, and compassion are born and, by the power of their inner attainment, rediscover and reinterpret the eternal truths of the religion in the light of changing social and economic mores. Indian Buddhism did, of course, produce great saints and sages even after the passing away of the Buddha; but, with its restricted demographic and geographical base, it simply was not strong enough to withstand the Islamic holocaust.

5. Light from the East

IKEDA: Having seen that such was the case, it is now time to attempt to examine the reasons why the urban intelligentsia formed the core of the Buddhist Order in India. As you know, an advocate of the equality of all people, Gautama Buddha opposed the caste system, teaching that deeds in this life and not heredity alone account for the human state.

His assertion, which is very much in keeping with the modern idea of total equality in the eyes of the law, made Buddhism, to an extent, a reforming, even radical, philosophy at the time of its inception. It must have been shocking to many. No doubt the conservative rural population, long accustomed to viewing human life in terms of fatalism, found it hard to accept Buddhist ideas.

The urban environment, however, is very different from the rural one. Cities always have a freer atmosphere than the countryside. Filled with the energy needed for creativity, they are a confluence of many cultural elements and stimulations. For this reason, they more readily accept the alien and the new, and through relations with these, urbanites evolve novelties of their own. People refine themselves in an urban environment, which vividly illustrates Arnold J. Toynbee's ideas of challenge and response between civilizations. The teachings of the Buddha were new and alien. For this very reason, the urban intelligentsia, lenient towards the foreign and curious about the new, possessed the intellectual powers to understand, and was the group most ready to accept, his teachings. Because of its reforming—I might even say modern—nature and because of historical and social limitations, Buddhism could develop only in the cities. (I am even tempted to say that it was far too advanced for its times.)

Today, however, when our understanding of humanity and life itself is very different and much more fundamental than it was in the distant past, not only can Buddhism find a wider understanding, but it must also be taught on the widest possible scale to help mankind find a way out of the impasse created by the deadlock the western philosophical approach now finds itself in, and in this way bring relief to our confused, perplexed age.

KARAN SINGH: As I have mentioned in earlier chapters, the Hindu view is not fatalistic. Nowhere have 'deeds in this life' been deprecated. What the theory of karma and reincarnation, in which the Buddha himself believed, implies is that our present situation is the result not of the fiats of whimsical divinities but of our own actions in previous lives. It follows that our actions in this life will inevitably mould the contours of our future. The divinity pervading all exitence was very much part of the Upanishadic worldview.

In some ways, not only Buddhism, but also the Upanishads were far in advance of their times. For example, the Vedantic view that a single divine power permeates all existence and resides in the heart of all beings is something that has, even today, not been accepted by large sections of humanity. Indeed the present human crisis flows from an inability to recognize the universal elements that lie behind both Hindu and Buddhist teachings.

The western philosophical approach has, until recently, been based on materialistic assumptions—what I call the Cartesian-Newtonian-Marxist paradigm. According to this worldview, matter is the ultimate basis of all existence and consciousness or spirit only an epiphenomenon. In the last four decades, however, this view has been gravely shaken by

Einstein's theory of relativity and subsequent developments including Heisenberg's Uncertainty principle; the theory of complementarity, quantum mechanics; and so on. The most recent research into subatomic physics and extragalactic cosmology has shown quite clearly that the materialistic paradigm is insufficient. Indeed some of the greatest scientists of our age including Einstein, Neils Bohr, Schroedinger, Prigogine, Jonas Salk, George Wald, and others recognize the fact that the insights of eastern religions express the newly discovered reality more accurately than prevalent western models. While the eastern view has still not been fully accepted by the western scientific community, I am certain that, by the end of this century, its acceptance will be widespread. In this context, I agree with you that Buddhism must be taught on the widest possible scale, but I say the same about the Hinduism.

IKEDA: I am certain that we both agree that eastern ideas, which fundamentally respect the dignity of life and prize spiritual matters, can shed light on and help resolve the current grave crisis that has come about because concern for such matters has been ignored.

6. Buddhism throughout Asia

IKEDA: During the thousand years (until the sixth or seventh century of the Christian Era) in which it centered mainly in the Indian subcontinent, Buddhism evolved into two main currents: Hinayana and Mahayana. As has been pointed out elsewhere, the term Hinayana (Lesser Vehicle) was first used by followers of Mahayana (Greater Vehicle) in deprecation of the Theravadins. Nonetheless, the two have now come into generally accepted, emotionally neutral usage.

In the most summary of descriptions, the Hinayanists can be described as concentrating on monastic practices, whereas the Mahayanists put most emphasis on lay believers. From its source Hinayana Buddhism spread mainly to eastern India, Sri Lanka, Burma and the Indo-China Peninsula. Mahayana

Buddhism, on the other hand, passed from western India into Gandhara, where it flourished before moving on, through Central Asia, to China, Korea and Japan.

Officially Buddhism entered China in the middle of the first century of the Christian Era. For centuries thereafter, priests from India or the Indian cultural sphere brought Buddhist scriptures into China and translated them into Chinese. The Lotus Sutra, the scripture revered by the branch of Buddhism in which I believe, was translated into Chinese in the early fifth century by Kumarajiva, a native of Kucha.

As the centuries passed and more and more scriptures were introduced, it became difficult to get a clear picture of the entirety of Buddhism or to understand Gautama Buddha's true intentions. In China, in the latter part of the sixth century, however, Zhiyi, also known as Tiantai (538–97), organized the teachings of Buddhism and clearly revealed their profound meaning. When this happened, Chinese Buddhism advanced from the stage of translation, annotation and introduction to a phase of systematized, independent faith.

After passing into Japan in the middle of the sixth century, Buddhism flowered into what was known as the Tempyo reign period in the seventh and eighth centuries. In the early ninth century, the priest Saicho (Dengy Daishi; 767–822) introduced the Tiantai teachings (known in Japanese as Tendai) into Japan.

Up to this point, Japanese Buddhism had been no more than a series of importations from China and the Korean peninsula. It was not until Nichiren Daishonin (1222–82), in whom I put my faith, that a system of Buddhist faith was actually created in Japan.

Such, briefly, was the northern development of Buddhism. Now I shall say a few words about development in the south. The immense Buddhist monument at Borobudur, Java, was built in the eighth century; and Angkor Wat in Cambodia was built in the late twelfth century, at about the time when Sri

Lankan Buddhism passed into Burma. Not all Southeast Asian Buddhism was of the Hinayana variety. Mahayana teachings entered Cambodia and Vietnam. In such places as Java, Buddhism combined with the worship of Hindu gods in an esoteric blend. And Theravadin teachings spread into Sri Lanka, Burma and Thailand.

As it was fading away or coalescing with Hinduism in India, Buddhism was spreading and flourishing in China and various regions of Southeast Asia. In other words, it ceased being exclusively Indian and, transcending national, racial and cultural boundaries, began manifesting its true nature as a universal religion for all humanity.

Esoteric Buddhism, or the so-called Vajrayana, which is said to be part of neither the Mahayana nor the Hinayana currents, arose in about the eighth century in India and passed from there into Tibet, China, and ultimately Japan. As I have said, it has influenced Buddhism in Southeast Asia.

Since it was essentially a fusion with Hinduism and therefore is strongly coloured with Indian culture, it is familiar to those who are accustomed to the Indian tradition. But I cannot help considering it alien to the true, essential nature of Buddhism.

Gautama Buddha rejected reliance on magical formulas and spells and taught that each human being should seek universal truth within himself and, relying on the Law (Dharma), strive to live in a wholesome human fashion. The esoteric Buddhist practice of relying on the power of mantras and spells seems to me to represent a throwback to primitive shamanistic practices.

I have even more doubts about such Vajrayana practices as asserting human instinctive desires, worshipping the female as a deity, demon worship, and the notion that enlightenment is to be attained through sexual pleasure.

KARAN SINGH: I find it difficult to enter into a value judgement regarding the respective merits of the Hinayana, Mahayana and Vajrayana schools of Buddhism, but am unable to accept your complete condemnation of Vajrayana, or *Tantric*, Buddhism. The human personality is far more complex and mysterious than is generally realized, and intellectual propositions and moral precepts are not always enough to satisfy the deepest inner cravings. Far from condemning it, I would look upon Vajrayana Buddhism as a most fascinating and creative development in which elements of Buddhism and Hindu tantricism are merged.

You seem to be startled at the link between sexual activity and spiritual enlightenment. May I point out that a whole school of Hindu thought, Tantra or Kundalini Yoga, is based on the hypothesis that the two are closely linked and that sexual energy can be transmuted into spiritual enlightenment. To those living in crowded cities this may appear a strange doctrine, but Vajrayana Buddhism arose not in urban centres, but in the windswept mountains of the higher Himalaya, where the ecology, the air, is quite different.

Vajrayana led to a truly remarkable efflorescence of art expressing itself in great *thankas* (scroll paintings), frescoes and sculpture. The entire Himalayan range is full of the most extraordinary artistic masterpieces, which are particularly impressive when one realizes that they have been created by Buddhist monks who have been isolated in those remote regions for generations.

In the Indian tradition, the origin of the Vajrayana school is traced to the great teacher Padmasambhava (eighth century of the Christian Era). The first European scholar with courage enough to rehabilitate the doctrine of Kundalini Yoga was Sir John Woodroffe, who wrote under the pseudonym Arthur Avalon. His extensive studies, which were published in the 1920s, threw tremendous light upon this hitherto obscure and widely misunderstood system. In more recent times, a Kashmiri named Pandit Gopi Krishna has written a series of books on this area including his remarkable autobiography *Kundalini*.

In the Hindu tradition, the Kundalini, or serpent power is a potent spiritual power believed to reside in the base of the spine. Under certain circumstances this power awakens and moves up the spinal column, energizing various centres, or *chakras*, in the process. It is believed that there are seven such chakras, which are successively activated as the Kundalini moves upwards. After piercing six chakras, the power floods into the cortex where the seventh chakra—the thousand-petal lotus—resides in the brain. When this happens, human consciousness is transformed and merges into divine realization.

All of this may seem strange and esoteric to people lacking exposure to even the teachings, let alone the experience. Nonetheless, it is an important element in the Hindu and Vajrayana traditions.

7. *The Influence of Buddhism on Indian Culture*

IKEDA: I have mentioned Buddhism's incorporation of elements from Brahmanism and now should like to hear your views on the ways in which and extent to which Buddhism has influenced Hinduism and other aspects of Indian culture.

KARAN SINGH: Buddhism has had considerable influence on Indian culture, and I have outlined some of the areas in which this impact has been expressed. Perhaps I should add here that the continuing tradition of Vajrayana Buddhism, which is an important element in the entire Himalayan range, provides a significant and colourful input into the vast and varied mosaic that is modern India.

As far as Hinduism itself is concerned, I have already pointed out that the Buddha is widely looked upon as one of the Avataras of Vishnu. While this may be unpalatable to many Buddhists, it does provide the two religions with a valuable harmonizing link of a kind that does not exist between Hinduism and either Islam or Christianity. On Buddha Jayanti day, millions of Hindus visit Buddhist temples and worship the image of Lord Buddha. Thus, in the rich and varied texture of Hinduism, the Buddha provides a valuable and valued dimension.

8. *Revival of Buddhism in India Today*

IKEDA: I understand that there is a movement in India today to re-examine the fundamental nature of Buddhism, apart from those esoteric Buddhist elements that have fused with Hinduism. In this connection, it is impossible to overlook the work of B. R. Ambedkar (1891–1956), although I realize that diverse views may be taken from the standpoint of politics or social movements. Born an 'untouchable', the most unfortunate of Indian classes, this brave man overcame an apparently insuperable fate to take a stand for the abolition of social discrimination. Of course, his abandonment of Hinduism was a step of great importance. But equally important was his conversion to Buddhism and his insistence that Gautama Buddha preached a doctrine of true equality, philanthropy, justice and independence. Going beyond this, he said that Buddhism is the only source of protection for the best in human nature.

I have heard that many people in sympathy with Ambedkar's views have converted to Buddhism. The number of Indian Buddhists is still very small, but what is your opinion of the future of Buddhism in India? What role do you think it can play in Indian society today and tomorrow?

KARAN SINGH: Dr B. R. Ambedkar was a remarkable figure in modern India. Generally, his major contribution is considered to be in the field of constitution-making. He was a brilliant jurist and played an important role in drafting and piloting through Parliament the Constitution of free India. He was Chairman of the Drafting Committee of the Constitution, and his great ability left a tremendous impact on the whole process. In fact he joined Jawaharlal Nehru's cabinet as Law Minister immediately after independence, but resigned after a few years as a result of difference of opinion.

The fact that he came from a Harijan background makes his achievement even more remarkable. Harijan, or Children of God, is the name that Mahatma Gandhi gave to the depressed castes who, in British times, were known by the odious term 'untouchables'. It is important to point out that, in order to make amends for their maltreatment in the centuries past, the Indian Constitution has incorporated special provisions for the welfare of Harijans and Tribals. The scheduled classes have job reservations of 12.5 per cent in all government vacancies, both at the central and state levels, and a similar reservation of 7.5 per cent is made for the tribal communities. Thus as many as twenty per cent of all jobs in India are reserved for these underprivileged sections. In addition, they enjoy preferential treatment in admission to educational institutions, promotions, and so on.

I mention this because Dr B. R. Ambedkar symbolizes the major role that the Harijans have played and continue to play in modern India. One of Mahatma Gandhi's great contributions was his implacable opposition to all forms of discrimination, and particularly to the undesirable tradition of 'untouchability'. It is a matter of great satisfaction that in the forty years of Indian independence, a major erosion of the pernicious custom of untouchability has taken place. While it may still be practised in some rural areas, the custom is no longer a major element in our social tradition. The credit for this must go to Mahatma Gandhi, Dr B. R. Ambedkar, and other stalwarts, including Jawaharlal Nehru, who moulded the contours of modern India.

With regard to Dr Ambedkar's conversion to Buddhism, it needs to be pointed out that, at the last census, there were about four million Buddhists in India. They fall into two categories: Lamaist Buddhists in the north and northwestern areas and a large number in the western state of Maharashtra. The latter belong predominantly to the Mahar community, from which Dr Ambedkar came, and adopted Buddhism after his conversion. Indeed his followers tend to look upon Dr Ambedkar himself as a divine personage, and his statue is installed in some temples. These people are sometimes referred to as neo-Buddhists or Ambedkarites.

In closing, may I remark that the radiance of Buddhism in India is not, to my mind, linked with the arithmetical number of Buddhists in this country. As I have pointed out in the course of this dialogue, the Buddha, his teachings, and his symbols are very much part of the Indian tradition and would remain so even if there were not a single Buddhist living in India.

CHAPTER FIVE

The Wisdom of the Orient and the Future of Humanity

1. Modern Civilization

IKEDA: All of the major problems facing modern civilization—the threat of nuclear war, exhaustion of Earth's natural resources, environmental pollution, moral degeneration, and so on—contain elements jeopardizing the continued existence of humanity. Although it is true that, at present, the industrialized nations are most seriously affected by these concerns, if they pursue material prosperity as their forerunners have done, the developing nations too will sooner or later have to confront at least some of the same problems. In other words, these problems affect all humanity.

Since these problems are man-made and therefore different from natural disasters, their solutions necessitate fundamental alterations in our way of living. And this in turn demands a profound spiritual revolution that will change our interpretation of ourselves and our surroundings. This is where oriental thought, which stresses the spiritual instead of the material aspects of human experience, becomes increasingly significant.

I am a Buddhist and you are a Hindu, and our religions differ in certain philosophical aspects. Nonetheless, both came into existence in India. And I believe that certain elements of Buddhist thought have been incorporated into and passed down by Hinduism.

Buddhism teaches that the Three Poisons of greed, anger and folly sully human life. Greed causes the desolation of nature and thus brings about such disasters as famine. Anger is the source of altercation and war, and folly causes both physical and mental illness. While teaching that these three poisons exist, Buddhism prescribes ways to purify life of them.

I am certain that such Buddhist teachings as these contain the key to the solution of the problems confronting humankind today. As a Hindu, how do you interpret the role of eastern spiritual civilization in dealing with the difficulties we now face?

KARAN SINGH: Mankind today is facing an unprecedented ecological crisis. As a result of rapacious exploitation over the last century, the biosphere has been gravely damaged. A nuclear holocaust would be the ultimate pollutant, destroying not only the human race, but also most other species upon this planet. Today it is necessary to remind ourselves that nature cannot be destroyed without mankind's ultimately destroying itself.

The curious notion prevalent in the West that the human race is in some way divinely endowed with sovereignty over nature—a notion that gives licence to destroy and pollute indiscriminately—is directly antithetical to the eastern worldview. Both Hinduism and Buddhism share the belief that mankind is a part of nature and that human welfare cannot be looked upon in isolation from the welfare of all beings. A purely anthropocentric view is unacceptable to us; we believe that all creation is divine, and this is repeatedly stressed in the Vedas and Upanishads as well as in many Buddhist texts, including the Lotus Sutra.

IKEDA: I would be interested to know whether there is a Hindu teaching corresponding to the Buddhist doctrine of the Three Poisons, which I mentioned earlier.

KARAN SINGH: Hinduism teaches that what are called the five major distortions—lust, anger, avarice, delusion and pride—are largely responsible for the disasters mankind has inflicted upon this planet. We share the view that these poisons can be eradicated only through individual effort and prolonged inner discipline. Unfortunately, governments magnify individual distortions a million times, making their resolution extremely difficult.

IKEDA: Yes, that is true. And this is the reason why, instead of allowing themselves to remain confined to their own special fields of interest, people of religion must find ways to apply their principles in actual politics and economics.

KARAN SINGH: It is my view that the eastern spiritual heritage can go a long way toward helping to solve the major problems facing mankind, providing the principles upon which it is based are widely accepted. Jawaharlal Nehru's Five Principles of Peaceful Coexistence (*Panchsila*) and repeated declarations by the Non-Aligned Movement (NAM) that insist on the importance of renouncing the use of force in settling bilateral disputes reflect the eastern attitude toward such problems.

It is necessary for us to work on two levels. Individually we must strive to reduce the effect of the so-called poisons within our own consciousness and in our daily activities. Collectively we must strive for a just and fair world based upon friendship and mutual respect. The key concept must be the unity of the planet Earth, which, in our traditions, is looked upon not merely as a mass of soil, stone and water, but also as a spiritual entity, the Mother that has nurtured consciousness for billions of years from the slime of the primeval ocean to the present human condition.

2. The West Turning Eastward

IKEDA: Although some people disparage it as a fad limited to a small number of eccentrics, the recent popularity of Yoga, the Hare Krishna religion and Zen Buddhism among young people in the West strikes me as clear indication of interest in oriental culture. As long as this interest fails to take root in ordinary living, however, it remains nothing but a hobby or a diversion lacking the power to work changes in the fundamental social and civilizational structure. And what we need today is not a mere diversion, but something capable of revolutionizing that fundamental structure.

The peoples of the West seem to have reached a point where they are questioning their own ways of thinking and living on the most basic level. What is your opinion of the current interest in things oriental among young Westerners? How would you characterize a spiritual civilization that is capable of offering leadership in matters related to actual, material living?

KARAN SINGH: The widespread revulsion in the West against the crass materialism that has dominated their civilization for many centuries has resulted in a considerable movement towards eastern religion and philosophy. This is no longer a fad; and a large number of people—young and old—are now turning towards Yoga, Zen Buddhism, and other eastern religious traditions. During my travels in the West over the past few years I have been greatly struck by the extent of this movement.

It is important to keep in mind, however, that the question is really no longer one of East or West, but one of a new global dimension. Mankind today is in a transition as fundamental as the earlier ones from nomadic to agricultural, from agricultural to industrial, and from industrial to post-industrial civilization. Science and technology have triggered revolutions in so many spheres, particularly communications and information technology, that, in our own lifetime, the world has been transformed into a global village. Unfortunately, there has been no commensurate transformation in consciousness, hence the dangerous gap between the emergence of a global society and its acceptance by the vast majority of mankind.

IKEDA: You are absolutely correct. Though the world is fated to be a communality, individual units within it remain isolated and plot war. It is as if people in a small room were threatening each other with explosives. The oriental concept that all beings should mutually assist each other can be useful in alleviating the tension generated by this situation.

KARAN SINGH: A significant number of people throughout the world strongly feel the pressure of the future and strive in their own ways to respond to our situation. The whole New Consciousness movement in North America and Europe bears testimony to this. Actually consisting of dozens of individual groups, this movement owes a great deal to eastern philosophy. The strange thing is that the East itself, which might have been expected to spearhead this transition to global consciousness, seems to have got mired in essentially western value systems and goals.

IKEDA: Practical affairs must be taken into consideration if a philosophy is to help people find new paths of thought and action. Although some forms of Buddhism can be accused of ignoring suffering in the present world and of demonstrating concern solely with post-mortem paradise, the teachings of the Lotus Sutra provide a way of revolution for the self and for all of society in actuality.

KARAN SINGH: To be valid and effective, a philosophy cannot neglect the material side of life. Hinduism is quite clear on this issue. It postulates four goals of life—Dharma, the framework of moral and spiritual values; Artha, material progress and well-being; Kama, sensual enjoyment; and, finally, Moksha, liberation. It can thus be seen that both material and sensual aspects are given due importance, provided always that they fall within the broad framework of Dharma and, ultimately, are transcended in Moksha.

3. The Lotus Sutra and Gautama Buddha's True Intentions

IKEDA: Since it was first compiled in India, I feel certain that you have had some exposure to the Lotus Sutra, the Buddhist scripture in which I put my faith and which was revered by the founder of Nichiren Buddhism, Nichiren Daishonin (1222–82), who described himself as its practitioner. I should now like to centre our discussion on this Sutra because I believe it contains truth that can help us solve the problems currently confronting humanity.

KARAN SINGH: Clearly the Lotus Sutra is not a text that can be grasped easily because it uses a wealth of imagery and expository techniques that must be understood before the deeper meaning of the Sutra becomes apparent.

IKEDA: Yes, as a matter of fact, the Sutra itself contains a comment to the effect that it is the most difficult to believe and the most difficult to understand of all Sutras that have been or will be expounded. In the early fifth century, Kumarajiva, of whom we have already spoken, translated the Sutra from Sanskrit into Chinese. Its Sanskrit title is *Saddharma-pundarika-sutra*; and its Chinese title in Kumarajiva's version is *Miaofa Lianhua-jing*, the Japanese reading of which is *Myoho Renge-kyo*, or the Sutra of the Lotus of the Wonderful Law. And, as the title suggests, the wonderful law is not easy to understand.

Though parts of it were compiled shortly after the death of Gautama Buddha, the bulk of the Lotus Sutra came into being five centuries later, at a time when, according to some scholars, an organized body devoted to its teachings may already have existed.

As you know, the Hinayana Buddhists, who stressed monastic disciplines, were opposed by the Mahayanists, whose teachings can be thought to emphasize salvation for the many. While recognizing the validity of both their approaches, the Lotus Sutra insists that everything is governed by one vast, all-inclusive truth and that rivalry between Hinayana and Mahayana should cease. Although some people have viewed the Lotus Sutra as exclusivist because of the way it rejects the idea of two separate, valid teachings, the principles contained in it are found in the so-called primitive teachings; and, at least, it can be said that the fundamental doctrines were the ones expounded by Gautama Buddha himself. The use of the word Sutra in the title indicates that it is one of the Buddha's teachings.

KARAN SINGH: The word Sutra in Hindu tradition means thread, the bare essentials of an exposition, memorized and handed down from generation to generation. The brevity and cryptic nature of such Hindu Sutras as Panini's Vyakarna Sutras or Patanjali's Yoga Sutras make them easy to remember. Each teacher explained the Sutra in detail; and some of their commentaries, called *Bhashyas*, are important to an understanding of the meaning of the texts. Thus the greatest Hindu philosopher—Adi Shankaracharya, who is believed to have been born in 788 of the Christian Era— wrote commentaries upon various key Hindu texts, which themselves became classics. The Lotus Sutra, however, is a long and complex text that lends itself poorly to memorization.

IKEDA: Actually the Lotus Sutra consists of passages of poetry, or gathas, interspersed with sections of prose usually of roughly the same content as the verse passages. It is thought that the gathas were transmitted by memory and that the prose sections, which contain commentaries and descriptions of conditions as well, were added when the Sutra was given written form.

Incidentally, the Chinese character used to write *jing*, for Sutra, in the title means thread, more specifically, the vertical thread, or the warp, in woven fabric, and is used in the names of such venerable, pre-Buddhist Chinese texts as the *Yijing* (The Book of Changes) and the *Shijing* (The Book of Songs). After the introduction of Buddhism into China, this character was used to translate the word Sutra.

The lotus, of course, has a very ancient tradition in India.

KARAN SINGH: In the Hindu tradition, the lotus has diverse spiritual significances. At the esoteric level, individual consciousness itself is often envisaged as an unfolding lotus; and the chakras, or centres, which are activated with the rise of the Kundalini power, are described as lotuses with a

varying number of petals. In Hindu mythology and iconography, the lotus is equally important. It is seated upon the
lotus growing from Vishnu's navel that Brahma creates the
universe. Again, the great goddess of grace and prosperity,
Mahalakshmi, is depicted standing upon a lotus and holding
a lotus in each of her hands.

To Hindus, the lotus represents the manifestation of the
divine and symbolizes purity and tenderness. Such of the
oldest Hindu scriptures as the Vedas and Samhitas are replete
with mention of the lotus as the seat or pedestal of Hindu
gods and goddesses. Sanskrit poets used the lotus as an
emblem of beauty to which they compared the faces of their
heroes and heroines. The lotus also entered into the art and
literature of other India-born religions like Buddhism and
Jainism. With the spread of Buddhism outside India, the use
of the lotus as an ornament in religious art extended to Sri
Lanka, Burma, Nepal, Tibet, China, Indonesia and Japan.

IKEDA: Although, in Chinese, Korean and Japanese art, too,
the form of the lotus blossom is frequently used as a pedestal
on which stand or sit various Buddhas and other figures from
the Buddhist pantheon, the true significance of the flower is
much more profound.

First, it is the famous symbol of the Lotus Sutra itself, in
which it stands not merely for a divine nature, but also for
the principle of the essential oneness of the life-force of the
unenlightened sentient being and the enlightened Buddha. As
the lotus blossom bears within itself its own fruit in the form
of seeds, so the sentient being contains within himself the
possibility of attaining Buddhahood in his current form.

In addition, since, though it grows in muddy waters, the
lotus puts forth flowers of immaculate beauty, the plant
represents the Buddha who, while living in the world of
delusion, remains undefiled by it.

KARAN SINGH: The same symbolism is effectively used to
illustrate the way a Hindu sage lives in this world. It is born
from the mud—hence one of its Sanskrit names, *pankaj*—and

lives in the water but remains detached and unaffected by its environment. Though in water, a lotus flower is always dry; and Hindu texts urge that we should all live in this mortal world (*samsara*) in such a way that, while fully involved in its activities, we still remain unsullied by the dirt around us.

The Lotus Sutra is one of the most popular Buddhist texts in East Asia, particularly in Japan, and is a pre-eminent scripture of the Mahayana philosophy. In India, the Dhammapada is generally better known as a definitive Buddhist text, but of late the Lotus Sutra seems to be gaining popularity. After commencing this dialogue I have had occasion to look through the Sutra; and, even on first acquaintance, it impresses me as a truly remarkable body of teachings expressed in eloquent and vivid imagery. In its original Sanskrit, a language of unparalleled majesty, it must be even more impressive than in translation.

IKEDA: I dare say that is true. But I should like to make a point about the nature of the content of the Sutra. Teaching that all sentient beings can attain Buddhahood, it embraces all humanity and is thoroughly egalitarian. It severely refutes Mahayana teachings denying the possibility of Buddhahood by means of both vehicles—Hinayana and Mahayana. In addition to rejecting the discrimination of the caste system in society at large, it eliminates discrimination between Hinayana and Mahayana within the Order itself. Although some people have criticized it as exclusivist, it must be remembered that, while rejecting discriminatory teachings, the Lotus Sutra is completely egalitarian where human beings are concerned.

KARAN SINGH: Nonetheless, it does explain the conflict and controversy that seem to have surrounded the followers of this Sutra, symbolized in a most dramatic fashion in the life of your great saint Nichiren Daishonin. His tempestuous career, full of trials and tribulations, is a remarkable saga.

IKEDA: Gautama Buddha denied the supreme universal truth

as taught by the Brahmans but also denied the teachings of the so-called Six Unorthodox Teachers, who opposed Brahmanism too. Looking hard at the actualities of human life, Gautama Buddha saw only inconstancy and void (*shunyata*), which led him to turn from both the orthodox and the unorthodox teachings of his day. It must be said, however, that the word shunyata does not imply nihilism but, as the primitive Buddhist texts repeatedly point out and as is made even clearer in the Lotus Sutra itself, stands for a middle way between being and non-being. I believe that the generosity and middle-way teachings of the Lotus Sutra represent Gautama Buddha's true approach. Nichiren Daishonin can be said to have manifested in his own life the truth revealed in the Lotus Sutra.

KARAN SINGH: You mention the word shunyata. This is indeed one of the most enigmatic and perplexing words in Buddhist philosophy. Etymologically it is derived from the root *svi* which means 'to swell, to expand'. Curiously enough, the word Brahman is derived from the root *Brh* which also means 'to swell, to expand'. This parallel is striking, because on the question of the ultimate reality hinges the whole basis of Hindu and Buddhist philosophy. Your view that shunyata implies a middle way between being and non-being, stands halfway between the concept of nihilism and the Hindu concept of Brahman, described in the Mundaka Upanishad as 'That which, shining, causes everything to shine; the light that illuminates the universe'.

IKEDA: Nichiren Daishonin manifested the truth of the Lotus Sutra in the form of *Nam Myoho Renge-kyo*. In relation to the Mundaka Upanishad, which you have mentioned, the Daishonin taught that everything, including all Buddhas, bodhisattvas, heavenly beings, and even mortal sentient beings in such states as those of hell and ravenous beasts, manifest their true and noble forms when illuminated by the light of the Wondrous Law. In other words, when they are fundamentally based in the Wondrous Law, all things in the universe, including human desires and greed, manifest their good aspects.

4. The Treasure Tower and the Dignity of Life

IKEDA: Although its initial part is set on the ground on Vulture Peak, the central section of the Lotus Sutra is a magnificent ceremony that occurs suspended in the air. A great assembly floats above ground to hear the teachings before a splendid Treasure Tower made of the seven precious substances, said to be as tall as the radius of the Earth is long.

As you have said, the sutras skilfully employ metaphor to make profound meanings easy to understand. And this apparently impossible Assembly in the Air and the vast Treasure Tower have a very deep significance.

Nichiren Daishonin has said that the Treasure Tower is the Mystic Law itself. No doubt, at the time of the compilation of the Lotus Sutra, the idea of erecting stupas to house relics of Gautama Buddha as objects of faith still persisted. Consequently, the appearance of the Treasure Tower, which is in the form of such a stupa, is not unexpected. The meaning of the tower in this instance, however, is different. The Lotus Sutra makes mention of erecting towers to house copies of the Sutra itself. In other words, emphasis is placed, not on the physical remains of the body of Gautama Buddha, but on the record of the teachings contained in the Sutra.

This interpretation clarifies the meaning of the magnificent incredible tower and the ceremony suspended in the air. This part of the Sutra proclaims the eternal life of the Buddha. In this instance, Gautama Buddha is not the historical Gautama Buddha but the Buddha of ultimate truth. It is therefore necessary for his teachings to be presented suspended in air, in clear distinction from those of the Gautama Buddha of history, who was subject to the limitations of time and space. The participation in the ceremony of the Tathagata Abundant treasure and of emanation Buddhas from all quarters of the universe symbolizes the universal nature of Gautama

Buddha's teachings, which are boundless in terms of both time and space.

The ceremony of the Treasure Tower is an expression of respect for the dignity of life, an issue of supreme importance in all ages. We must make constant, unflagging efforts to realize the dignity not only of our own lives, but also of all other life forms and to act in a way reflecting that realization.

Distinct from the historical personage of the same name, the Gautama Buddha who enters the Treasure Tower symbolizes the Buddha nature inherent in all sentient beings. This is why the Lotus Sutra stresses the nature of the tower, not as a container of relics, but as a receptacle of Sutras. It is not the individual Gautama Buddha, but the universal truth he represents, that is great. This truth pervades the universe and is the Buddha nature in all sentient beings.

And, if we translate this dazzling assembly into the terms of ordinary life, we must interpret the innumerable emanation Buddhas too as representations of the Buddha nature. The splendour of the tower can be viewed as the splendour of the universal force of life—it is so magnificent as to be compared in size with the whole Earth itself.

Nichiren Daishonin drew a parallel between the seven precious substances used in the tower and the following acts of human faith: hearing the Law, believing and keeping it, abiding by the precepts, meditation, diligence, joyful giving, and repentance. Human beings manifest supreme value when engaged in these practical activities in the pursuit of Enlightenment.

KARAN SINGH: The amazing description of the Assembly in Space in the Lotus Sutra is indeed fascinating. It reminds me of the great *Vishwarupa Darshan*—Vision of the World Form—which Sri Krishna reveals to Arjuna on the battlefield of Kurukshetra, and which represents the most dramatic portion of Hinduism's best known text, the Bhagavadgita. Like the Assembly, the Gita's vision is of the resplendent, multifarious universe in all its bewildering diversity unified in the form of a great spiritual revelation. Indeed a comparative study of the Bhagavadgita and the Lotus Sutra could yield much valuable material.

Such unique phenomena as the Assembly in Space or the World Form can be interpreted on different levels. There is the intellectual interpretation, like the one you have given regarding the Assembly and the Tower. This is important, especially for the rational and intellectual elements in our consciousness. Then there is a symbolic interpretation, whereby each of the substances making up the tower can be compared with certain virtues and each of its levels can be taken as representing various aspects of the teaching. Such creative symbology can often throw unexpected light upon aspects of the teaching that might not be immediately available in a purely rational interpretation. There is yet another way of viewing these phenomena: to look upon them as states of inner consciousness or, better still, as expressions of enhanced states of consciousness. Great teachers like Sri Krishna and the Buddha have the capacity to transmute the normal waking consciousness of their disciples into realms of dazzling beauty and majesty. These interpretations are by no means mutually exclusive; human consciousness has many levels of awareness, and great texts such as the Bhagavadgita and the Lotus Sutra operate on several levels simultaneously.

In your remarks regarding the Assembly in Space and the vast Treasure Tower, you say that the message is that all sentient beings possess inherent Buddhahood in the form of the Buddha nature and can come to understand universal truth, which is Life itself. As a Hindu I would be quite prepared to accept this, interpreting Buddhahood as the light of the all pervasive Brahman and Buddha nature as the undying Atman within each individual.

IKEDA: In all ages, awakening to the value and dignity of life, which is expressed by the Assembly in Space and the great Treasure Tower in the Lotus Sutra, is a matter of utmost concern for all humanity. Of course, ceaseless efforts must be expended in the name of respect for not only one's own individual life, but for all other life forms as well.

While claiming to honour the dignity of life, modern civilization is often so strongly governed by desire and impulse that, in our highly organized society, the individual human life tends to be reduced to a minor part in a great machine. I am firmly convinced that, under such circumstances, the respect for life set forth in the chapter on the Treasure Tower in the Lotus Sutra and efforts to awaken people to the need to honour life's dignity are of the greatest significance.

KARAN SINGH: I am in full agreement with you regarding the danger of the individual's being steamrolled in present social and political organizations. In our own century we have seen how collectives of different kinds—economic, social and political—have reduced millions of human beings to mere ciphers in the name of what is claimed to be the larger interest. It is here that the Hindu-Buddhist view of the dignity of the individual is significant. In the Upanishads, human beings are referred to as children of immortality, implying that each individual has the right to develop his or her inner consciousness until it bursts into the glory of spiritual realization. Hence each individual is precious and unique, and his individual dignity must be respected.

5. Significance of the Eternal Life of the Buddha

IKEDA: The eternal life of the Buddha, a highly distinctive concept of the Lotus Sutra, cannot be understood apart from the ancient Indian doctrine of transmigration, or samsara. In Buddhist doctrine, the serene state of Nirvana is liberation from this cycle. In contrast to the modern idea that rebirth into this world is desirable and filled with hope, ancient Indians found life an aggregation of sufferings and sorrows into which rebirth was anything but welcome. And for this reason they longed to break the chain of transmigration.

KARAN SINGH: The concept of rebirth over vast periods of time until the soul finally attains Moksha, or liberation, is a fundamental tenet of Hinduism. Samsara is looked upon as a state to be transcended, not because it is necessarily full of suffering as we understand it, but because worldly pleasures cannot last.

IKEDA: In other words, the state of samsara must be overcome to attain liberation (Moksha), the condition that may be referred to as Nirvana.

A Buddha is one who has escaped to Nirvana. If this is so, however, the Lotus Sutra teaching to the effect that Gautama Buddha has been a Buddha since the infinite past runs counter to the teaching of Nirvana, for if a Buddha has broken from the chain of transmigrations why should he be born again as a human being into this mortal world, as Gutama Buddha was?

The concept of the eternal existence of the Buddha, therefore, was a reversal of approach towards the idea of transmigration, which, instead of being something to escape from, becomes desirable truth to be welcomed. In this respect, the Lotus Sutra is by far more positive in outlook than the other Sutras.

KARAN SINGH: It is important to remember that, in the Hindu view, the period between births in this world is spent either in pleasant or in unpleasant states according to one's own karma. Good karma gains good after-death states and favourable rebirth conditions, but the Upanishads are insistent that even the most ecstatic heavenly enjoyments are evanescent and fleeting when viewed in the longer time span. It is for this reason that the cycle of birth and death is to be transcended. There is, however, less emphasis in Hinduism upon suffering than there is in Buddhism, because the Buddha postulated his entire philosophy upon the assumption that life is nothing but suffering, dukha: while Hinduism holds that the essence of life is bliss, ananda.

IKEDA: The astronomical figures used to represent infinity in the Lotus Sutra—and especially frequent in the latter half—signify that, by this stage of the text, the Buddha is no longer the historical person Gautama Buddha, who was born in India, but is Gautama Buddha as a manifestation of eternal Buddhahood. In other words, emphasis has shifted from the finite, historical Gautama Buddha to the infinite, true Gautama Buddha. The doctrine of the eternal life span of Gautama Buddha indicates that he is himself an eternal Buddha and that the Buddha nature exists infinitely and is accessible to all sentient beings. In other words, the Buddha is not a creator-god exercising sway over humanity, but is an infinite, ubiquitous Buddha nature existing in all beings.

This is a source of great hope for people born into the world after Gautama Buddha's death and unable, therefore, ever to come into direct contact with him. But, if the Buddha is truly an entity demonstrating compassion equally to all sentient beings, his life force must be eternal and immutable. By demonstrating that such is indeed the case, the Lotus Sutra enables sentient beings born after Gautama Buddha's death to make, not only the revealed truth, but also this compassionate entity, their mainstay.

KARAN SINGH: The concept of the eternal nature of the Buddha is a very striking one and reminds us of the great declaration by Lord Krishna in the tenth and eleventh chapters of the Bhagavadgita. Considering the manner in which the Buddha is shown in the Lotus Sutra as transcending space and time and encompassing a whole range of beings from the celestial to the subhuman and of all ages from the distant past into the illimitable future, it is quite clear that the Sutra represents the Buddha no longer as a historical person, Prince Siddhartha, but as a symbol of the eternal Buddhahood. If life is to have any meaning, the divine principle must transcend time and space, and must be reflected within all beings.

The issue of a being who has transcended birth and death, like the Buddha, poses the question you raise: why was he born at all if he had already achieved liberation? The answer to this question is that, once he attained illumination, he became what one would call a *jivanmukta*, and his *future* births would take place only as a result of a deliberate act of his own will. The purpose of his being reborn is to save people. This brings us one of the most important contributions of Buddhist thought: the concept of the Bodhisattva, a great being who, having achieved Nirvana, turns his back on ultimate bliss and, instead of merging into the great ocean of light, takes upon himself the burden of serving humanity by sweetening the bitter sea of sorrow. There is a similar concept in the Upanishads, but Buddhism highlighted this aspect, which emerges as one of the most impressive features of the Lotus Sutra.

IKEDA: The Indian prince Siddhartha was a partial manifestation of the Eternal Buddha; and, as is set forth in the Lotus Sutra, Bodhisattvas who emerge from within the Earth itself appear in this wicked world to save sentient beings after the death of Gautama Buddha.

In addition to being the fundamental source of all things in the universe, the eternal Buddha nature exists in the life of each sentient being. The Lotus Sutra stresses this universality. Tracing the existence of the Buddha to the infinitely distant past simultaneously clarifies the Buddha nature's spatial boundlessness. Furthermore, showing that the Buddha, who was formerly considered distant and isolated, actually abides within all sentient beings, has a limitlessly elevating effect on humanity.

The Buddha cannot be truly universal unless he exists within sentient beings. And such a universal existence is precisely what the Lotus Sutra emphasizes. Its view of the Buddha is infinite in terms of both time and space. And making the holy and distant Buddha a living entity within sentient beings elevates us all to infinite heights.

KARAN SINGH: What you call the Buddha nature is what we in Hinduism call the personified aspect of the Brahman, the

Great Being that stands behind all manifestation and that descends in human form from time to time in order to spread the spiritual Dharma. Both in Hinduism and Buddhism there are predictions that in the present cycle, or *yuga,* there will be one final such manifestation before a major catastrophe destroys the world—the *Kalki Avatara,* or Maitreya Buddha.

IKEDA: While recognizing the eternal nature of life, Westerners posit a final judgment, after which will follow either unending bliss in heaven or unterminating torment in hell. Unwilling to accept this mythlike interpretation of existence after death, however, modern human beings tend to fall into the belief that life is a one-time affair, at the conclusion of which comes only nothingness. I consider this attitude a fundamental threat to respect for the dignity of life.

KARAN SINGH: With regard to the Semitic notion of a single life followed by an infinitely long period in heaven, hell or purgatory until a final judgement 'at the end of time', I agree with you that this seems to be a most unsatisfactory position. It gives enough time for neither the fulfilment of karma, nor the flowering of spiritual realization within the individual. I often liken the idea of a single life with a child being sent to school for only one day but being expected to cover a full educational course in that day. Further, the Semitic position offers no acceptable explanation for the immense diversity of the human condition, in which millions wallow in dirt and poverty while others live off the fat of the land.

IKEDA: I agree entirely. Only in the light of a philosophy positing eternally repeated existences in which karma is worked out on the basis of the law of cause and effect is it possible to explain the apparently inexplicable disparity in human conditions. In addition, it is important to remember that, instead of being helplessly bound to fate, we are endowed with the great power to challenge and alter our karma. While limited by the same desires and instincts as other animals, human beings have and must cultivate the will-power, reason, and ethical sense to overcome those restrictions.

6. *The Buddha Land and the Cosmos*

IKEDA: The Lotus Sutra mentions the assembling of emanation Buddhas from all quarters of the universe to hear the teachings. This raises several very interesting points.

First, this means that Buddhas exist in the Three Worlds of the past, present and future, and in all directions; that is, they are ubiquitous in terms of space and infinite in terms of time. In other words, a limitless number of Buddhas inhabit a limitless number of worlds. This means that the world we human beings inhabit is in no way unique but merely one of an immense number of worlds. The view of the cosmos represented by this approach is vastly different from those of most religions, which assume that this world, the planet Earth, is the only world there is and that it has its own Heaven, which is likewise unique.

KARAN SINGH: Although the teaching found in the Lotus Sutra symbolizes the universality of the Buddha's teachings, the concept of an infinite number of universes—*anantakoti brahmanda*—is deeply rooted in the Vedas and was also adopted in Buddhism. The term *Brahmanda*, means the universal egg. And, indeed, seen in a photograph, the Milky Way, floating in cosmic space looks like a huge egg. Hindu cosmology is most beautifully portrayed in the great figure of Shiva-Nataraja, the Lord of the Cosmic Dance. In one hand he holds the drum, which symbolizes the creative power of the World, impelled by which millions of universes spring into existence without end. In another hand he holds the fire, which symbolizes the destruction of these worlds. With a third hand he preserves creation and comforts his worshippers, while with the fourth he points towards his upraised foot as indicating the path of salvation from this cycle of creation, preservation and destruction. The dancing figure is surrounded by a nimbus, which symbolizes the cosmic dimension.

In much of Buddhist iconography, these myriad universes are represented in various ways, and therefore I would not say that the concept of an infinity of worlds is confined to the Lotus Sutra.

IKEDA: I see; but, in the Lotus Sutra, the aim is not to expound this view of the cosmos but to set forth the eternal and universal nature of the Law and the Buddha's greatness. Explaining the space-time limitlessness of the Buddha world implies that, since truth is universal, enlightenment to it, too, has no space-time limitations. This can be interpreted as a statement to the effect that the Law is always the fundamental source of Buddhism.

KARAN SINGH: The Hindu view is that there have been in the past, not only in this solar system, but also in millions of other worlds, an infinite number of divine manifestations and that there will be infinitely more in the future. Until recently this view was laughed out by western philosophers, but now that radio astronomy has shown that there are hundreds of millions of stars in our own Milky Way and hundreds of millions of galaxies in the observed universe, scientists are beginning to look upon our tradition with greater respect.

IKEDA: Advances in the natural and physical sciences are making it apparent that the views of the world, the cosmos and matter based on oriental philosophy and religion are closer to the truth than many of the ideas here-to-fore held in the West. This is true partly because, since oriental religions are much less dogmatic than Judaism and Christianity, it has been possible in the East to take a more objective view of the world. Of course, many aspects of oriental thought on these matters have been very shallow.

KARAN SINGH: On the other hand, many deserve to be re-evaluated by science. A persisting, curiously conservative body of opinion stubbornly insists that the tiny speck of dust

that we call Earth is the only place where human consciousness has evolved or to which the divine has descended, but
this view is so absurdly egocentric that it will be unable to
hold the field much longer. It is to be hoped that, by the end
of the century, this attitude will have become as outmoded as
that of the Flat-earth society.

IKEDA: I believe that philosophical and religious truth has as
much universal applicability and communality as the fundamental truths elucidated by the sciences. The countless
emanation Buddhas, who have come to the assembly from
the infinites of time and space, bear witness to the truth of
the teachings of the Lotus Sutra and thereby indicate that this
truth is universally applicable. Consequently, I feel certain
that beings as sophisticated as, or possibly more sophisticated
than, human beings inhabiting other worlds in cosmic space
would at least fundamentally agree with the law of cause and
effect in life and with its ethical ramifications.

KARAN SINGH: It is, of course, a moot point as to whether
exactly the same law would be applicable in all these millions
of worlds. Certainly, as you say, the law of cause and effect,
or karma, however, would seem to be universal. It is just
possible that, because of our intellectual limitations, we tend
to project our present knowledge and concepts on the
universal scale. Let us remember that what were once called
'immutable laws' governing the behaviour of matter break
down once the scale becomes either extremely small or
extremely large. It is quite possible that some orders of
beings may exist who are free from the law of karma, just as
the law of gravity, which appears immutable on this planet,
in fact ceases to function outside the gravitational sphere.

7. Reinterpreting Delusion

IKEDA: A major teaching of the Lotus Sutra holds that
delusion and wisdom are actually one and the same thing. By
delusion (klesha) is meant those things that cause suffering
and pain to the human mind; that is, desires. In contrast to

the Hinayana insistence that we must strive to divest ourselves of them, the Lotus Sutra teaches that we should convert desires into enlightenment and wisdom. The Sutra of Meditation on the Bodhisattva Samantabadhra, regarded as the concluding section of the Threefold Lotus Sutra, comments on not breaking with delusion and the five desires. Most ancient Indian philosophy, including pre-Buddhist Brahmanism, regards delusion as an evil.

Gautama Buddha was enlightened to the truth that all things in the universe are interdependent and rely on each other for existence. This is why Buddhist philosophy teaches that, to the maximum of our abilities, we human beings should make every effort to repay all other things for the good we enjoy from them; and this means that we should love all things. Doing so is especially important in times like our own.

KARAN SINGH: I find the approach of the Lotus Sutra in this regard to be creative and compassionate. Instead of stressing the sinful nature of man, as some of the great world religions tend to do, the Lotus Sutra is a great declaration of faith in the inherent goodness of human beings. We must, however, admit that delusions or, rather, ignorance can cause havoc. In Hinduism the concept revolves around ignorance (avidya) rather than sin (papa). The great ninth-century Hindu philosopher Shankaracharya holds that, when the divine knowledge is born within the human psyche, ignorance is automatically dispelled just as darkness disappears with the rising of the sun. The awareness of our limitations and a determination to overcome them are an essential feature of the spiritual quest, and the interpretation of the Lotus Sutra in this regard is indeed a positive one.

As far as our individual delusions are concerned, once we have realized that they *are* delusions, the problem resolves itself. But the real difficulty arises when people refuse to accept that they are deluded. There is a saying in India that it is possible to wake someone who is sleeping, but it is impossible to wake someone who is pretending that he is asleep, because, however much we may shake him, he will refuse to open his eyes. This is the attitude of those who consider themselves wise, when in fact they are mired in ignorance. Of such does the Upanishad speak when it describes 'the blind leading the blind.'

IKEDA: Unbridled desires—or delusions—may be considered reprehensible when they hinder the absolute harmony that should prevail in the world. Instead of attempting to make repayment to other life forms for their help, however, human beings allow their own ugly, selfish desires to exploit and harm them. This is an example of disrupting universal harmony. Moreover, because of the law of cause and effect, acts of this kind inevitably rebound on the perpetrator. In other words, they are a source of suffering for human beings and for all other forms of life.

If correctly used, however, human desires can be oriented toward compassion for the life-forces of other living forms and toward the preservation of universal harmony.

The Lotus Sutra assertion that delusion (desire) and wisdom are one can be interpreted in the following way. While it can become an evil force destructive of the universal harmony, human delusion can, if founded in a higher wisdom, contribute to the preservation and strengthening of that harmony. In other words, it is possible in this light to take a positive view of humanity.

The Lotus Sutra teaches that, instead of allowing ourselves to be swayed by delusion and its associated desires and instinctive impulses, we should strive to develop ourselves into independent, tough-willed human beings capable of wisely using our own delusions and desires in the correct way. This seems to me to be the most important issue facing humanity.

KARAN SINGH: Another way of viewing this problem, which could be called the evolutionary approach, has been brilliant-ly expounded in recent times by the great Indian philosopher and yogi Sri Aurobindo. In his powerful and dynamic philosophic structure, the key concept is the evolution of human consciousness. According to him, man today, though at the peak of the evolutionary pyramid on this planet, has by no means reached ultimate growth. He is in fact an intermediate creature, somewhere halfway between the animal and the divine consciousness, and his spiritual destiny lies in taking the next evolutionary step from the mental to the supermental level. According to Sri Aurobindo, this step alone can really enable the individual to overcome delusion and to get a correct insight into reality. The method of this transformation, which he calls Integral Yoga, has been worked out by him in great detail and is expounded in his numerous works, including *Life Divine, The Synthesis of Yoga,* and *Essays on the Gita.*

From the Christian point of view, a somewhat similar exercise was undertaken by the great Jesuit philosopher Teilhard de Chardin, whose major work *The Phenomenon of Man* was, significantly enough, proscribed by the Roman Catholic Church and published only after his passing away. I mention these evolutionary philosophers because their approach has a direct bearing on the problem of mental delusion. While certainly one must take a compassionate view about delusions, it must be quite clear that the inner quest seeks to overcome, not perpetuate, them.

8. Reincarnation and the Dignity of Life

IKEDA: Although it is probably universally accepted that respect for the dignity of life ought to be the foundation of society, peoples in the East and the West take different views of the object of that respect. Acting on the basis of the Old Testament teaching that man was the ultimate creation of God, who was given sway over all other creatures, Westerners generally consider human life worthy of maximum respect. The oriental tradition, on the other hand—and it is especially strong in India—is that human beings ought to live in harmony with all other life forms. In both China and Japan, animals are customarily deified or feared for the superhuman powers they are believed to command.

At the heart of the oriental attitude towards other animal forms may be discerned the doctrine of reincarnation—which is incorporated in Buddhism too. According to this teaching, though human at the present time, under the influence of the good or bad karma accruing during life, an individual may be reborn in either human or non-human form. Eastern peoples subscribing to this doctrine therefore consider it wrong to treat cruelly other animals that conceivably might be reincarnations of relatives or loved ones. Similarly, they consider it natural to be compassionate and helpful to other human beings who, though strangers now, within the boundless flow of metempsychosis, could be the reborn forms of parent, sibling or spouse.

I believe that this attitude towards all forms of life is essential to modern human beings, who often tend to be excessively individualistic and self-centered.

What is your interpretation of the difference between the eastern and western attitudes towards respect for the dignity of life, and the significance of that difference?

KARAN SINGH: In September 1986, a unique interfaith meeting was held in Assisi, Italy, in which the attitude of five great world religions towards the relationship between man and nature was studied in depth. This exercise resulted in the preparation of five statements on behalf of Hinduism, Buddhism, Judaism, Christianity and Islam. Despite the sharp divergence with regard to reincarnation between the Hindu–Buddhist tradition on the one hand and the Semitic tradition on the other, it was fascinating to see the close convergence in all these declarations regarding the necessity for reverence to all living creatures, including animals and plants.

The key would seem to lie in the concept of an all-pervasive divinity, whether looked upon from the eastern standpoint as being immanent, or from the western standpoint as being part of 'God's creation'.

For those who are not particularly attached to any religious tradition, including millions of Communists, the whole question can be posed in a non-theological manner by stressing the importance of preserving the ecological balance.

Indeed the ecology movement in the United States and the Green movement in Europe, which have developed over the last few decades, show quite clearly that the western assertion that human beings enjoy absolute sovereignty over this planet is rapidly being challenged by a more caring and compassionate viewpoint. From the broader angle, it is essential that mankind move away from the obsessive anthropocentricity that has characterized western civilization over the last several centuries, and adopt a wiser and more enlightened attitude towards all existence.

IKEDA: As far as reincarnation is concerned, unavailability of objective information on pre-life and post-mortem conditions hinder universal acceptance of the doctrine. But I should like to hear your opinion of ways in which we can further stimulate awareness of the dignity of all—not just human—life.

KARAN SINGH: While it is unlikely that the Semitic religions will theologically accept the concept of reincarnation, although increasing numbers of individuals are moving towards this view, it should nevertheless be possible to awaken devout Westerners to an appreciation of the dignity of non-human life forms by stressing the divine element behind creation.

Whether or not the phenomenon of reincarnation, or life after death, can be proved to the satisfaction of the doubters, the awareness of the interconnectedness of all things must grow, while the core of individuality remains intact. Thus what is really required is a creative fusion between the best in the eastern and western traditions for the sake of a benign holism that alone can ensure the welfare of the planet Earth in this nuclear age.

9. The Wisdom of the East and the Future of Humanity

IKEDA: In the earlier phase of the modern period, developments in science and industry, and great material power enabled certain European nations to subject much of the Orient to the cruel sufferings of imperialism. Now, having experienced, through two global wars in the twentieth century, the horrors to which material might can lead, Europe has been reduced to a supporting player in the tragedy of conflict of power between the Soviet Union and the United States and the threat of total annihilation of the human race.

Though now independent of the European yoke of imperialistic control, all but a very few of the new nations of Africa and Asia remain too economically weak and politically unstable to pursue courses of truly independent development.

It is true that the problems faced by the Soviet Union, the United States and Europe, and those of the nations of Africa and Asia are different. Nonetheless, all humanity shares a common fate and must now pool its powers in the struggle to overcome the difficult problems confronting it and build a brighter future.

India and the Orient in general have a spiritual culture that can contribute greatly to the future of humanity. But to enable eastern peoples to manifest their strengths in this connection, steps must be taken towards the solution of pressing issues of poverty and social unrest. The populations of China and India are far greater than those of the Soviet Union and the United States. In addition, with their thousands of years of cultural tradition, these nations could occupy positions of great leadership in the world. I am convinced that India's growth and contributions to the world could enormously influence the nations of Africa and Asia. I should like to know what future developments you foresee for your nation. Furthermore, I should like to ask you to define the kinds of efforts we peoples of India, China, Japan and other eastern nations should make in applying the profound wisdom of our traditions for the sake of the future of humanity.

KARAN SINGH: It is true, as I have reiterated in the course of this dialogue, that humanity today faces the gravest challenge it has ever known. The proliferation of nuclear weapons, and the continuing confrontation between the United States and the Soviet Union—not to speak of lesser conflicts in other parts of the world—pose a serious threat to the very future of the human race and indeed to all life on this planet. By its very nature the threat is such that the nations of the East, including India, China and Japan, are, willy-nilly, faced with equal danger.

This is a time when the wisdom of the East could once again give a creative turn to the human condition, and there are three major lines upon which this should proceed. Firstly, the attitudes of the Asian countries towards nuclear proliferation must be clarified. If, as seems likely, a race for nuclear weapons begins in Asia, we will hardly be in a position to lecture western nations regarding nuclear disarmament. This is an area in which public opinion must be mobilized so that the urgent problems of providing the minimum needs of our peoples are not swept aside in a renewed burst of military spending.

Secondly, regional initiatives within Asian communities must be aimed at settling bilateral issues in a peaceful manner. This will go a long way towards releasing much-needed resources for the amelioration of poverty in Asia and will greatly strengthen the Asian position vis-à-vis the western powers. Thirdly, there must be Asian initiatives—if possible supported by some western nations—to help bring about a rapprochement between the United States and the Soviet Union. The recent Six-Nation Peace Initiative is a good step in that direction.

While, essentially these three areas must be dealt with by the concerned governments, it is necessary for the peoples of all the Asian nations to rebuild among themselves those links of understanding that languished during the colonial period. As a consequence of centuries of foreign domination, India and Japan, for example, know much more about the United States than they do about each other. A dialogue such as the one we have undertaken can be looked upon as a small contribution to the generation of mutual knowledge and understanding.

In the final analysis, it is in the minds and hearts of human beings throughout this planet that the bulwarks of the new consciousness must be built. In concluding this dialogue, therefore, may I express the hope that the ideas we have articulated will create a ripple effect that will help in forging the new globalism to which both of us are deeply committed.

Index